A WHOLLY OWNED SUBSIDIARY OF **TBN**

PROFESSIONAL PUBLISHING MEETS POWERFUL PROMOTION

Trilogy Christian Publishers

A Wholly Owned Subsidiary of Trinity Broadcasting Network

2442 Michelle Drive

Tustin, CA 92780

For information, address Trilogy Christian Publishing

Rights Department, 2442 Michelle Drive, Tustin, CA 92780.

For information about special discounts for bulk purchases, please contact Trilogy Christian Publishing.

10 9 8 7 6 5 4 3 2 1

Library of Congress Cataloging-in-Publication Data is available.

ISBN#: 979-8-89333-127-1

ISBN#: 979-8-89333-128-8

Table of Contents

Prologue:

In 2019, after a diagnosis of Multiple Sclerosis, I began praying for what the Lord wanted from me. What should my response be? The only thing I heard was "Rest and Write." So, I began writing a blog. I thought of it as an open journal, a place to write down my thoughts, conversations, or encouragements from the Lord as I walked through this new trial. I heard from heaven, and I was encouraged.

The hope He gave me has sustained me and given me the rocks I needed to stand firm through this. In this book, I am sharing what He showed me through the trial so far and the encouragement He has given me. This is a book of devotions and a peek into my conversations with the Lord.

My hope is that in my struggle, others will see the hand of the Lord carrying me through, and I pray this will be an encouragement to anyone walking through the same illness or anything similar.

Let me say, if you have been recently diagnosed, you are not alone, and you CAN fight this! Your Father in Heaven loves you with a perfect, unending love, and His will for you is healing. I pray that on your journey you uncover every hidden injury and find complete restoration. I believe, at least with me, that the underlying cause of autoimmune disease can be traced back to unresolved internal injuries that cannot be treated with medication. We need His healing, His understanding, and His revelation to truly find restoration from this type of injury. God doesn't only care about healing you physically. He is interested in your complete restoration.

If you have a loved one who is battling this or something like it, and you are lost for how to help them, know this: By aligning yourself with God's perfect plan for your own life, you will take a massive burden off your loved one and that alone can begin the healing process for them.

My goal is that you find hope here. You will see that our humanity is not repulsive to Jesus, and you will be encouraged that even in the darkest spaces, the Lord is there with you.

Chapter 1

About MS

Here's what I have learned about the disease since my diagnosis. Multiple Sclerosis is a degenerative, debilitating, progressive disease with no known cure. The first documented case was noted in the mid-1800s. Until recently, there has not been much offered in the way of treatment. Now, there are various diets and drugs out there offered as treatment, but not cures.

It is considered an autoimmune disorder where your immune system thinks your nerve lining, called myelin, should be attacked and removed. The wearing away of the myelin sheath causes misfirings in your central nervous system, which then cause debilitating symptoms such as numbness, tingling, heaviness in arms and legs, ocular degeneration, vertigo, brain fog, back pain, and imbalance. In the worst of cases, MS can cause the loss of use of limbs, bodily functions, blindness, and a whole host of other symptoms, depending on where those lesions occur. It is a progressively debilitating disorder.

As you can imagine, receiving a diagnosis like this is not the easiest thing to deal with. I've always been a very active, healthy person all my life, and this disease attacked everything I identified with. I could no longer do the things I was used to doing. I'm tired a lot. I can't eat what I want to without it causing a flare. I can hardly walk sometimes, among other things. My neurologist said, "There's nothing really that will make you feel better," but offered DMTs (disease-modifying therapy) to keep the lesions at bay.

My personal choice initially, after much prayer and deliberation, was to not do the recommended drugs because of the potential side effects and their lack of long-term progress and efficacy. Deciding whether to take medication is an incredibly personal choice and

I fault no one for going either way with it. This was MY personal choice that I prayed about and the only option I felt peace about.

Here's what I know: God still heals today, and He will heal me. Right now, I'm on my way to healing, just like I'm on my way to heaven. If I can believe God to save my soul from hell, then certainly I can believe Him to heal my body and walk with me through this. The question I have to ask myself is, do I believe that He is sovereign?

No matter the trial, I can trust that God's intended end is for my good and His glory.

Why?

1 Peter 4:12-13 says, "Beloved, do not think it strange concerning the fiery trial which is to try you as though some strange thing happened to you; but rejoice to the extent that you partake in Christ's sufferings, that when His glory is revealed, you may also be glad with exceeding joy. (NKJV)

Chapter 2

God's Faith in Us

Did you know God also has faith in us? I know there is a specific and individual work that God is doing inside of each of us, and usually, He is doing way more than we even know.

Job, in his testing, questioned God. Even his "friends," who seemed to be men of God and had knowledge of God, rebuked Job. Maybe that's a whole different topic, but I'll say, we can't expect people, even close friends, to understand completely the testing we're walking through and even the most seemingly godly people can be wrong.

Job's testing was very specifically targeted towards him. All his things, his children, and his health were ripped away from him. His own wife was consumed in negativity. Imagine, your own spouse, the person who knows you best, is consumed with hopeless negativity, completely disgruntled, and tells you to curse God and die. She was sick of seeing him suffer, and this was her solution.

Job, in his humanity, was understandably miserable and regretted the day he was born, but he never cursed God.

But God's faith in Job is what is astounding to me. He allowed Satan to test Job, knowing that he would not curse Him. Knowing that he'd lose all he lost, his wife would discourage him, and his closest friends would rebuke him, but God knew that Job would keep his faith in Him.

How many times are we told, "Just have faith in God, and He will help you?" Though I believe that's true, it stands out to me that God had such faith in Job. He knew Job would defeat his enemy, enduring the fiery trial he endured.

"Have you considered My servant Job," God asked.

He knows us by name, and He knows our hearts. Job had a servant's heart. The very first chapter tells us how Job would go and sacrifice for his children in case they might have sinned. God, knowing and believing in Job, allowed him to face this trial. The intended end for Job was complete restoration, even greater than before the testing.

Job's reward was reserved in the heart of God from the very beginning and given to him after the testing.

"After Job prayed for his friends" is worth noting. How hard is it to pray for someone who has misjudged you and even blamed you for your trial, your illness, financial situation, marriage issues, whatever the trial? But it was "after Job prayed for his friends," that his reserved blessing was given to him. God help us.

How encouraging is it to know that God believes in me, too! He allowed this trial not to hurt me but to grow me, to bless me, to encourage somebody maybe. He had enough faith in me to say, "Yes, she can handle this; she will overcome, and My blessing is reserved for her!"

If my trial points to Jesus and glorifies Him, then it is worth it!

"For I consider that the sufferings of this present time are
not worthy to be compared with the glory which shall be
revealed in us."

Romans 8:18 (ESV)

Chapter 3

The Theme of My Heart;

Living Above the Noise

"My heart is overflowing with a Good Theme." Psalm 45:1
(NKJV)

I ran across this scripture and thought, I have never noticed this before. My heart has a theme. I started thinking how impacted my perception of life's situations would be by my heart's theme. I had never considered my heart having a theme. I see it as a filter of the things that come into my heart. When things come into my life, and then into my heart, how are they processed?

Are they coming through a filter of discouragement, anger, disgruntledness?

Or are they coming through a filter of hope, love, mercy, compassion, and kindness? You know, all the fruits of the spirit.

What happens to the things we see and hear when we allow them to enter our hearts?

What do we do with them?

What are they mixed with in our hearts, and how do they come back out?

I read a story about the blind beggar in Luke, Bartimaeus. The bible says in Luke 18, when he heard the commotion in the crowd, he asked what it was about, and they told him that it's Jesus of Nazareth. So, he cried out, "Son of David, have mercy on me." Those who were leading blind Bartimaeus warned him to be quiet. Nevertheless, he cried out all the more.

He knew He was the Coming One, The Messiah. He calls Him, "Son of David." Bartimaeus knew this was the promised king. His heart was expectant.

But he had to overcome the noises around him.

1. There was the crowd. 2. There were the voices of those who went before him.

How did he discern this was his Jesus moment and his time to be healed?

He asked those around him what the commotion was about, and they told him it was Jesus. So, he had the word he was told. But they warned him to be quiet. Now, he also had discouragement, but in his spirit, he knew to "cry out all the more." His heart's theme was ready for Jesus.

The bible says that Jesus stood still and called him to be brought to Him, and when he came near to Him, Jesus asked him what he wanted from Him. So, the blind man, discerning his moment and having the faith that if Jesus said he was healed, he would be healed, when he was brought near to Jesus, replied, "That I may receive my sight."

What if he had received the discouragement in his heart when he was warned to be quiet? Or what if he had not asked what the noise was about? He could have died as a blind man. Jesus told him, "Receive your sight; your faith has made you well."

This is a noisy, NOISY world. There is so much noise out there that if we fail to discern or look for Jesus in the noise, if we allow the discouragement to alter the theme of our heart, we'll miss what God wants to do.

Examples of NOISE

One of the first things I noticed with this illness is the utter crookedness of the healthcare industry. I do not understand everything about the ins and outs of it, but I know it's messed up.

When I was diagnosed, the doctor recommended I immediately start medication. I was told that within 5 years, I would likely be in a wheelchair if I didn't begin treatment soon. The treatments varied from $6,000 to $18,000 per infusion or dose. This, along with steroids and yearly MRIs, bloodwork, office visits, etc., would quickly add up.

When I went in for my initial MRIs, I was terrified. I had no idea what was going on with my body. I could barely walk or stand. The $3,800 charge per MRI (I had 4 of them) to my insurance at the time would have only cost me $900 if I had gone in as Self-Pay and not presented any insurance to the provider.

This just triggered a recognition of the type of greedy world that we live in, and this situation brought a lot of disappointment to me regarding this industry. I don't know what I was expecting. The corruption in that world is no secret. Nevertheless, it was disappointing to walk through and is an example of the type of discouraging noise we can be faced with.

It's not just the Healthcare Industry. I worked for a financial institution for 10 years from 2005 to 2015. For those of us who remember the financial crisis of 2008, it was interesting to have been a financial industry employee during that time.

I saw bankers, financial advisors, lenders, etc., come and go. I got to a place where I could recognize those who were what we called "upwardly mobile." It was easily recognizable who was about the money, not the people. I could usually recognize malintent within a few minutes of a conversation.

It was unfortunate. I would watch as adult children were rapidly dwindling down their parents' life savings. People were liquidating 40 years of investments on the promises of higher returns, advisors were promising no risk, "safe" investments where the explanation and understanding of the underlying products were misrepresented. All for the love of money.

It's not just one industry; it really is the theme of our hearts individually.

Sad.

Noise.

All the coming and going brought me to this conclusion. People will ultimately do what is best for themselves, and shouldn't they? And why is that disappointing? Should it be?

I think it boils down to what satisfies the theme of their hearts. They will endure a job, a situation, a commitment, or a relationship if it is convenient and beneficial for them. But over and over, I saw how quickly someone moved on once they no longer benefited from the circumstances.

Our world is overcome by greed, and it really can be so discouraging if my heart's theme is one that welcomes offenses, anger, and all the ugly that's out there. Because if we're not careful, we'll see situations where the love of money is king and who is involved, and we'll allow this discouragement into our hearts.

Who can say that they've continually endured a detrimental situation to themselves for the benefit of others? And does that make someone greedy?

No.

Greed is loving money with no regard for the detriment of others. God loves for His children to prosper, so it's not about money. It's about what you allow to be sovereign in your life.

What can be said of these things?

Jesus tells us not to worry when the wicked prosper in his ways. Yes, big pharma is making boatloads of money, and yes, the banks and financial institutions are too. Of course, big business is in it to win it, but what does the bible say about riches?

The bible says it's a sad situation when a man trusts in riches and not in God. "If riches increase, do not set your heart on them." Psalm

62:10. (NLV) He wants us to be so secure in our faith in Him that we recognize riches for what they are, a kingdom resource, and we recognize Him for who He who is, above it all.

God forbid we see the prosperity of others as a threat to ourselves and allow it to cause an offense in us. Who can save a soul with money?

"Those who trust in their wealth and boast in the multitude of their riches, none of them can by any means redeem his brother, nor give to God a ransom for him."

Psalm 49:6 (NKJV)

Salvation cannot be purchased, and God cannot be bargained with. God isn't about finances; He's about salvation. Jesus wasn't concerned with Bartimaeus' money because he had none. He was concerned with his faith. "Your faith has made you well." What offering can be made to God that can redeem a soul?

Everything already belongs to Him.

"For the earth is Mine and all its fullness."

Psalm 50:12 (NKJV)

"The sacrifices of God are a broken spirit and broken and contrite heart."

Psalm 50:17 (NKJV)

Humility and thanksgiving. Yes, provision is something He promises, come on ravens! But He is more concerned with the theme of our hearts.

Is it one that is turned off by the noise, one that is offended at the prosperity of others, one that misses the Jesus moment when He comes walking right past us?

Or is it one continuously looking for Jesus in the crowd, listening for Him in the noise, and willing to be louder than the noise of discouragement all around us?

Is it one that sees this state of the world as an opportunity to be gracious, loving, and compassionate to those who need to be brought near to Jesus so they can hear Him say, "What can I do for you?"

I can be responsible for what I allow to affect the theme of my heart. If I want to receive what I need from the situations I encounter, I need to be diligent about maintaining my heart to keep it "overflowing with a good theme."

Chapter 4

I Mean, What Did I Expect?

Life is learning, right? Someone asked me, "If God loves you, how can He sit back and watch you suffer like this?"

I try, really TRY, to live a sinless life and pursue excellence in everything I do. I ask the Lord to check my heart often because I honestly want my heart to be right with Him. This is what I desire, and it's how I try to live. Now, do I mess up? Oh yeah. Why? I don't know, I guess it's just part of being a human.

I've learned so much since embarking on this journey with MS, and I know there's so much I still don't know. The pain and discomfort I experience can be vastly different from someone else with the same diagnosis.

The central nervous system is extremely complicated, and if you don't believe in creation, I implore you to start digging into the complex workings of our brains, bodies, and systems. It's not hard to see how intricately designed we are. If I believe I was so "intricately designed," what part can I play in my healing?

That said, I felt like, in some cases, I was blamed for getting this disease; like the way I was living or something I "allowed" caused me to open the door to infirmity.

Okay, I'm open to exploring that. If I have, and this is what I said to the Lord, "If I have opened a door to this Lord, expose it so I can repent and be rid of it." But it can hurt your feelings to be accused of opening doors to evil when you're just trying to live right.

Okay, so maybe you didn't open the door to sin; perhaps, "you're just overworking yourself and you haven't taken the time you need to focus on God and seek His rest."

This was true, but did I thereby invite illness into my body? Was me getting MS my own fault? Everyone has an opinion of what you're going through, you know. So, how do I answer that question? Why is God allowing this?

Does the question imply that it's God's fault that I'm sick? God, who I believe designed my body in and out. Could that question also suggest that there is an error in His creation? If it's His fault I'm sick, then He somehow messed up when He made me because something is going wrong.

MS is an autoimmune disorder where your immune system, designed to fight illness, attacks your nervous system, your actual nerve lining. So, what did I have to do with that? I didn't design my immune system.

"Well, you weren't careful with what you ate," and "you got stressed out easily." I've heard my share of opinions lately and have gone in circles of thoughts.

But is it anyone's fault?

Is the answer I did or didn't do something that invited the infirmity, so I'm getting what I deserve?

Is the answer God isn't concerned with the pain I'm in?

Is He teaching me a tough love lesson?

I honestly don't know the answer.

What I know is what the word says, "Surely there is a hereafter." So, anything I face here on earth will pass away and what if someone sees me lose hope, and gives up their fight? Or, what if someone sees me have hope and they keep going?

I CAN make that decision.

I also know healing is a promise that Jesus Christ, Himself died for.

"He was bruised for our iniquities, the chastisement of
our peace was upon Him, and by His stripes we are (I am)
healed!"

Isaiah 53:5 (NKJV)

So why am I still sick?

Is it my faith that is lacking?

I know I'm saved, but I'm not in heaven yet. I still have a purpose
to fulfill on this earth, and the Lord is using this illness to fulfill that
purpose for my good and His glory.

When I asked Him to use me, what was I expecting? A chariot
ride to heaven? Elijah was an outcast for years. People wanted him
dead. But his obedience destroyed the greatest threat to God's word
during his time, Jezebel.

I know God's word to be true. I'm given an opportunity to live out
what I believe through this trial. If I ask to see God moving, "Lord,
let me see Your activity," if I ask Him to use me however He wants,
"Lord, have Your way in my life," then shouldn't I be grateful for any
opportunity like this to show others that even through illness, God
is Good? Can He be anything but good?

Should a Christian be without struggle?

Where would gratitude for provision come from if I never knew
lack, or for healing, if I never knew illness, or for restoration if I
never knew brokenness, or deliverance if I never knew bondage?

What was I expecting?

God wants us to look to him during these trials, but not only
during the trials. He wants us to look to Him every moment of every
day. Let me leave this chapter with this thought; What did you expect,
and who did you expect it from?

People will always disappoint you. They are people. Even the
most well-intended remark or deed can bruise you. I've noticed the
greatest disappointment will come from those whom you hold in the

highest regard. Comments like those coming from someone close to you, or a pastor or mentor surely can push you back a few steps.

Maybe they didn't respond to your situation as you thought they should. But what were you expecting and from who, and why?

Our misplaced expectations can only lead us down a road to offense, and if we're running from God and blaming Him for the trial we suffer, what hope can we have for His intervention?

This trial is not my fault, and it's not God's either. But it will be used to glorify His name and point others into His arms. I don't doubt His love for me. I don't doubt His plan. He is everything I need. He is A GOOD, GOOD FATHER.

Let me run into His arms.

"He who dwells in the secret place of the Most High shall abide under the shadow of the almighty. I will say of the Lord, "He is my refuge and my fortress, My God. IN HIM I WILL TRUST."

Psalm 91: 1-2 (NKJV)

Chapter 5

Triggers

I found out the hard way that stress exacerbates MS symptoms. Many of us who have found this out try desperately to manage triggers and keep them as far away as possible. I'll use Aleve, CBD cream, or oil (non-THC) for pain, but seems like the only thing that helps with stress is removing or fixing the triggers.

Messy house stressing you out? Clean it. Feel better. It works.

Not resting? Rest. It works. (If I can).

But I never really thought of myself as "high-strung" or easily stressed out, and those people who I thought were I stayed away from because, honestly, they stressed me out and I do not enjoy being around negativity. I never thought I'd be the kind of person I would myself avoid.

I struggled with this when my stress level started affecting work because I knew there was an entire church depending on me: children, parents, volunteers, pastors. I needed to "get it done."

I knew the Lord wanted me to rest early on, even before I was diagnosed. He said, "Come away, by yourself, and rest a while." I couldn't understand it when He highlighted the scripture.

When was I going to rest with all the stuff that I needed to do? I didn't know how to stop.

I noticed the stress increasingly affecting my physical body, causing stiffness, pain, and irritability.

At first, I didn't realize these were symptoms. It wasn't until I sort of came to grips with the diagnosis and began researching the disease that I found out more and more about stress triggering and exacerbating symptoms.

Being the way I am, I would get angry at myself for not living up to the standards I felt were expected of me, which only made the whole situation worse. After a while, I got to a point where (this will sound dramatic, but it's how I felt) I felt like I would die if I kept going like I was. So, I stepped down from the role I was in and for the weeks following, I attempted to rest.

This was incredibly hard. I have always worked. I didn't know how to rest, or what *resting* meant. I desired to be obedient to the call to rest, and now, with my health concerns, working was no longer an option. I expected the Lord to provide, but I saw our financial situation. I couldn't understand why we continued to struggle despite the promises of abundant life in scripture that I professed to believe in.

God makes us promises, and when you know the word, you know God's promises. But, I thought, He says I will bless the work of YOUR hands. So, I struggled with this because I know He also told me to rest.

It's hard to "rest" though, when you're not bringing in a paycheck, and the entire load falls on your husband, who's literally working his every waking hour, so I can "rest," and it feels like climbing up the wrong way on an escalator.

How can I rest? I felt tense even writing this. It's not fair to him. I felt like I needed to do something. But resting was something, right? I don't know. This is where faith comes in.

I believe He's going to heal my body; I believe He's going to save my soul. Surely, I can believe for our needs to be met. But was there something I could do to help financially that wouldn't stress me out?

My husband did it as gracefully as possible, but I knew it was weighing heavy on him. So, I looked around for some things I could do from home or freelance for extra money to help, and I tried not to be super negative about things he was into that he's spent money on.

This was super hard because I saw our financial struggle.

I just got to where I was calling for abundance: "Open the windows of heaven, Lord." Right. "The earth is Yours and all its fullness. Go ahead and open them up."

I'm very open with the Lord. He knows my heart and thoughts anyway. I just asked for His help all around. "Help us be good stewards, make the right decisions, be responsible. Just help us, Lord."

Maybe there was a mindset I needed to get to. I have these expectations of people, and situations, and even God. When I don't see them measuring up to what I know they are capable of, it's like I become internally injured. I'm callous and closed off outwardly. Like, "Fine! It's fine. I'll just do whatever "it" is by myself. Because I know I can depend on myself."

But inside, there's turmoil that only the peace of God can subdue. Newsflash, I don't get to tell God how and when to come through for us. That's the thing when you follow someone; you can't see what's in front of them. You see what's in front of you, which should be Him.

How do I walk in that peace, that rest? That perspective? He knows what lies ahead of me. I just need to trust Him and remember He has good things in mind for us.

The worst thing my kids can do is complain to me. It immediately stresses me out. "Oh, what you have isn't good enough? Want me to show you broke?" You know? "I'll take the internet away." First-world problems.

We went to an open house for my daughter. They had a book fair going on. She wanted a book and a puppet. $26 later, she leaves the library with her new stuff. We meet the teachers, and some kids have these new sparkly water bottles that they gave away. So, she wants one. We leave and look for where they were giving them out, and they're all out. So, she goes home completely bummed out and pouting because she didn't get a new water bottle, even though she has 2 brand new items in her hand. I cannot tell you how frustrated I was; well, yes, I can; it really ticked me off. "I just dropped $30 on you, sister. Who cares about the water bottle?" But still, I felt bad she didn't get one.

I expected her to be grateful. And still do. I expect God to come through, and He will. But I know He expects me to be grateful. His Son died for me; no matter what I go through, this is the lens I need to see through. The lens of His love, grace, and mercy.

Lord, help me not be ungrateful. We are very blessed. We're not hungry; we're clothed, warm, and safe. I should be grateful. I am, and I don't mean to sound otherwise.

God has a way of bringing me back down to humility. I'm so thankful for the word. My husband shared with me that he had been reading in Habakkuk. So, I read it and came across this:

"Though the fig tree does not blossom, and there is no fruit on the vines, though the yield of the olive fails, and the fields produce no food, though the flock is cut off from the fold and there are no cattle in the stalls, yet I will [choose to] rejoice in the Lord; I will [choose to] shout in exultation in the [victorious] God of my salvation! The Lord God is my strength [my source of courage, my invincible army]; He has made my feet [steady and sure] like hinds' feet and makes me walk [forward with spiritual confidence] on my high places [of challenge and responsibility]."

Hab. 3:17-19 (Amplified)

When the challenges are hard, my intentionality towards praise should be all the more loud. Even in what I think is lack, He promises courage, strength, surefootedness, and confidence; He is my invincible army. "Whom shall I fear?"

It's been a hard week, but God is faithful and will come through for us. I get to choose how I go through these challenges. And it won't be in anger and bitterness when rejoicing is one of my options.

I CHOOSE to rejoice. It's a choice, my choice.

Chapter 6

Covering or Criticism

I journal a lot, like 5 subject notebooks full of my thoughts, notes, and prayers. Mainly prayers and revelations that I live by. I was looking for some paperwork we needed, and I came across a message I had sent to a friend, and it triggered a thought I wanted to share.

Remember Noah? When he settled on the mountain after the flood, he planted a vineyard. One day, he got drunk, and one of his sons found him naked and passed out in a tent. The first one who found him thought it was an opportunity to dishonor his father, and left his father there uncovered, then went and told his brothers how he found his dad. The other two brothers came and went backward into the tent and covered their father's nakedness.

"The sons of Noah who came out of the ark were Shem, Ham and Japheth. (Ham was the father of Canaan.)[19] These were the three sons of Noah, and from them came the people who were scattered over the whole earth. Noah, a man of the soil, proceeded[a] to plant a vineyard. [21] When he drank some of its wine, he became drunk and lay uncovered inside his tent. [22] Ham, the father of Canaan, saw his father naked and told his two brothers outside. [23] But Shem and Japheth took a garment and laid it across their shoulders; then they walked in backward and covered their father's naked body. Their faces were turned the other way so that they would not see their father naked."

Genesis 9:18-24 (NIV)

How I wish we would treat each other like the second boys, not the first. Cover each other's nakedness. Noah represented a lot, but

I want to point out that God called him a man worth saving. Out of all the families on the earth, Noah's was the only one saved from the flood.

Then Noah got drunk and passed out in a tent. What? He was supposed to be chosen by God. He was a father. He was a prophet. He was God's messenger. He did what! What a terrible example, right? Maybe Ham had a right to go and tell his brothers like that because Noah messed up, right?

I don't think so. The problem was Ham left his father in his nakedness. He didn't even try to cover him. He left him there, exposed to go and tell on him.

Parents, husbands, wives, preachers, prophets, teachers, whoever, no one is exempt from this thing called humanity. But what heart do we show when we see someone's weaknesses and use it as an opportunity to ridicule and judge them.

Here's what I want to ask; That person who offended you, have you prayed for them even once?

In their weakness that you saw, did you even try to cover them?

Have you asked God to check your own heart to see if there may be something that needs His grace and mercy?

How many times was Saul vulnerable before David, but David dared not raise his hand against him. He even defended him because he was God's chosen one at that time. Saul literally tried to kill David over and over, but when we read David's prayers, He asks God to be his vindication, and he asks God to check his own heart.

I wish we would let God be God and worry about our own hearts more than letting what seems to be a weakness in others be an excuse to ridicule and bash them. I told someone the other day when we see weakness or faults in others, it's an invitation to introspection (plank in the eye) situation, not a "look at you messing up" situation.

The second two sons covered their father's nakedness. That's what we are supposed to do: cover each other in prayer, grace, and compassion. David knew Mephibosheth was lame, but he sat him at the king's table and covered his lameness.

Let your pastors live in nice houses; let them buy what they're going to buy. Let your husband or kids mess up when they do. Let them make the decisions they make. Let them be human because, guess what, they are. I can't control the decisions others make. What I can control is what I allow to offend me, and I can choose not to be offended when someone makes a mistake.

Pastors, husbands, teachers, mothers, fathers, and those in authority- yes, they do have a higher responsibility, and most of them know it, but they, like all of us, will answer to God. GOD. Not me. My position is to pray for them.

I need to assess whether a thought or comment is coming from a place of covering or from a place of criticism. I'm too messed up to judge anyone. Pray for your spouses, pray for your pastors, pray for your teachers and mentors, and pray for yourself.

"As for me, I will be satisfied when I awake in Your likeness."
Psalm 17:15 (NIV)

Chapter 7

I Just Want to Sleep

I don't talk to many people about how I am "really" doing. Sure, I get asked all the time now, "How are you feeling?" But usually, it's in passing, and most of the time neither one of us really has the time to go into it. So, I say something like, "I'm good, you? or "I'm fighting the fight." or "Hanging in there." or my favorite, "I'm fine, Thank you! How are you?"

The honest answer lately is I'm barely holding it together. Putting one numb foot in front of the other, almost like a robot. I hurt all the time; my feet and legs feel like they're being squeezed constantly; my lower back hurts, even feels tight, and I can't sit, lay, or stand any way that will make it better. It doesn't go away, not even for a moment.

But on the outside, I look completely fine. I have been extremely discouraged and searching every minute for a little hope, but really, all I want to do is sleep, because when I'm sleeping, I don't know I'm in pain, and I don't feel the discouragement, and maybe I'll dream of something better.

I have so much compassion for anyone with a chronic illness, whatever it is. Imagine being in pain and discomfort, constantly with no hope of relief at all.

I really don't know if it's possible to understand how pain can lead to depression unless you experience it, but I pray you never do. It's agonizing. It's not necessarily the symptoms; it's the thought of "When will this ever go away? How long, Lord?" And knowing there are people around me who see this as something I've caused myself adds to the agony.

If I believe in healing, then why am I not healed, and why are the symptoms spreading? Why are we still behind? Where are my promises, and where is the evidence of my faith?

I know this is a moment, not a final destination, so in that I remind myself there is hope. Casting down every vain imagination, yes, I know. There is reason to have hope, and I know it's all perspective. I do have so much to be grateful for. This is just how I've been feeling.

We went to a new neurologist last week. He is a smart guy. My husband liked him, which says a lot. He showed us my images up close and, in detail, explained all the spots on my brain, the scarring, and the more dangerous lesions throughout my spinal cord and how those affected my movements and the potential for long-term damage.

"I was only diagnosed in July," I reminded the Dr. "How could I have so much scarring?" He told us that I've had this disease for 15 years, easily. Additionally, the weakness had then spread to my left side (which, obviously I did notice, but my neurological exam showed the abnormalities).

So, it has been rough lately. Because I was hopeful that the super strict diet, supplements, not working, etc., was actually doing something, and yet, the weakness was spreading, hence the discouragement.

My husband was doing what he knew to do. Work. But I knew it was wearing him thin, and I was still not working. I looked for things maybe I could do, but honestly, I feared getting into something and immediately having to step down. I hated how stressful all this was.

My sister shared a scripture with me, John 5.

"Sometime later, Jesus went up to Jerusalem for one of the Jewish festivals. ² Now there is in Jerusalem near the Sheep Gate a pool, which in Aramaic is called Bethesda[a] and which is surrounded by five covered colonnades. ³ Here a great number of disabled people used to lie—the blind, the lame, the paralyzed. [4] [b]5 One who was there had been an invalid for thirty-eight years. ⁶ When Jesus saw him lying there and learned that he had been in this condition for a long time, he asked him, "Do you want to be made well?"

"Sir," the invalid replied, "I have no one to help me into the pool when the water is stirred. While I am trying to get in, someone else goes down ahead of me." Then Jesus said to him, "Get up! Pick up your mat and walk." At once the man was cured; he picked up his mat and walked.

John 5:1-8 (NIV)

I know of the story, so I thought on it a bit and moved on with my week. I ran across a video where the preacher spoke on the same scripture. I liked the video, but I just kept thinking about this man. The more I thought about him, the more I felt like this guy.

He tried over and over to get himself into the healing waters, but he could never get there. Every time he got close, someone went in before him. He thought he needed to be healed the way everyone else was experiencing it, so he kept trying to get there. He just needed to get into the water. But when Jesus found him, the bible says, he was just lying there.

What happened?

Why was he just lying there and not trying to get to the water?

It seemed so easy for Jesus to heal him. But Jesus asks, "Do you want to be healed?"

I would ask Jesus, "If he didn't want to be healed, why was he even there? Why did he try and try to make his way to the healing water over and over?"

Did Jesus really wonder if this man wanted to be healed?

Or was it more like, "Will you let Me heal you?"

"Will you let Me heal you in a way you're not expecting?"

Because he had in his mind, he would be healed in a certain way (by getting in the water), but Jesus came and challenged everything he thought he knew about how he would be healed.

I can imagine this man probably every time he could muster up hope, got up and made his way towards the water, each step, picturing how he'd come out: "If only I could get there, I could be healed." And oh, the cold disappointment when another got in before him, and over and over again, he missed it. "Failed again! Why do I even try!"

I wonder if he felt like I did. "I'd rather just sleep; I'm so tired of hurting; I'm done being sick; I'm tired of being disappointed." I wonder if that's how Jesus found him, just lying there in his sadness, disappointment, and discouragement.

Did he even hope at all anymore?

Or was he just lying there, so discouraged that when Jesus encountered him, He knew he needed to be reminded of the hope that was there for him?

"Do you want to be made well?"

Maybe Jesus was getting the man to remember his faith, to declare, "Yes! I want to be healed." Maybe he needed to remind himself that he still wanted healing and he could still believe for it. Maybe Jesus was reminding him not to give up on his faith for healing.

"When Jesus saw him lying there and knew he had been in that condition a long time, He said to him, "Do you want to be made well?"

How many times did He say, "Your faith has made you well"?

I think this man had given up, but Jesus knew he needed to be reminded of his faith. If he could just be reminded there was something to hope for, and he would say it out of his own mouth, he would get his healing, and if he could get to the place where he was open to "however" Jesus wanted to do it.

Is it after I've given up all hope that He comes, or is it when I stop thinking I can have anything to do with it and accept that maybe God has something for me that I haven't seen before?

Was the man even expecting Jesus to come for him? Was Jesus just leisurely passing by, or did He intentionally seek him out to heal him?

Lord, help me to be open to whatever You have for me and not think anything must look or be a certain way.

My hope is in Him. However, You do it, Lord; I say, "Yes, I want to be made well."

Chapter 8

Relax Already

At the beginning of this month, I said I'm declaring this a year of good news. A preacher told our church this year (on the Jewish Calendar) is, "The year of the mouth," which means declaration. The bible says, "Man shall be satisfied by the fruit of his lips." So, guess what, if it's good, I'm declaring it. Favor, provision, healing, all... the... things.

Recently, I was talking to someone who has entered a new season where provision is more abundant, and the temptation is to proceed cautiously in case, you know, the ball drops. Like, "Well. I knew that was coming." It's like we almost expect to be let down, so it may soften the blow if disappointment shows up. We need to be more okay with the good that comes into our lives. It's like we're afraid to enjoy the good that comes our way in case something happens, and we lose it.

Why not expect good, and what's wrong with enjoying those seasons? Not sitting on the edge of the last season, waiting on it to creep into your new one. How can we enter the rest available there if that's where we stay?

In the last few weeks, my husband got a new job paying $4 more per hour (working when he wants), a couple handed us a 4 THOUSAND DOLLAR check to help us catch up on our back mortgage payments, my neurologist found a medicine that could help keep MS from progressing that has less severe side effects than the others initially offered, and that I won't have to pay for including the baseline and follow up MRIs, and I have a new potential job lined up that I can do without it being too hard on me. With all this going on I should be jumping for joy, but I find myself also "proceeding with caution, just in case..."

I've been reading Max Lucado's book *When the Angels Were Silent*. He tells about the workers who were hired at a certain wage. There were those picked first and paid for the day, then He went and got more workers and paid them the same and went back again later grabbed more workers and paid them the same, and so on till the end of the day. He pointed out the ones picked first were likely the strongest and most able, and the ones picked last were likely the most feeble and unqualified, yet they all received the same wage. His point was that the reward was available for all of them regardless of when they were chosen or the hours they were putting in.

James 1:17 says,

"Every good gift and every perfect gift is from above, and comes down from the Father of lights, with whom there is no variation or shadow of turning." (NKJV)

and Proverbs 10:22

"The blessing of the Lord makes one rich, and He adds no sorrow with it." (NKJV)

Someone shared a scripture with me this week, Psalm 21:

"The king shall have joy in Your strength, O Lord; And in Your salvation how greatly shall he rejoice! [2] You have given him his heart's desire and have not withheld the request of his lips. Selah [3] For You meet him with the blessings of goodness; You set a crown of pure gold upon his head. [4] He asked life from You, and You gave it to him. Length of days forever and ever. [5] His glory is great in Your salvation; Honor and majesty You have placed upon him. [6] For You have made him most blessed forever; You have made him [a] exceedingly glad with Your presence. [7] For the king trusts in the Lord, And through the mercy of the Most High he shall not be [b]moved. [8] Your hand will find all Your enemies; Your right hand will find those who hate You. [9] You shall make them as a fiery oven in the time of Your anger; The Lord shall swallow them up in His wrath, And the fire shall devour them. [10] Their offspring You shall destroy from the earth, And their [c]descendants from among the sons of men. [11] For they intended evil against You; They devised a plot which they are not able to perform. [12] Therefore You will make them turn their back; You will make ready Your arrows on Your string toward their faces. [13] Be exalted, O Lord, in Your own strength! We will sing and praise Your power." (NKJV)

So, we ask the Lord for goodness, life, and strength, and then He gives it to us, His blessing, because we trust in Him, even the desires of our heart, He gives us. And what do we do sometimes?

Well, I hesitate to enter the joy of the blessing for fear of something bad happening. I stand on guard just in case I have to start fighting,

But as I'm reading this, I'm reminded that God's goodness is HIS for me and belongs to me. He gave it. I remember that it's only because He is merciful that I receive it. Not because I am the strongest, most able, or deserving. It's only because I am His chosen.

How sad is it when I give up the joy found in the blessings of salvation for fear of a coming enemy?

The scripture gives me an image of enemies all around when God's people have found His blessings, and the enemies are on the way to steal everything good God has for us. Still, the picture I see here is God Himself, standing as my guard with His bow out and His arrow drawn, ready to hit the enemy in the face if it even tries to come near us.

"They devise a plot which they are not able to perform, You will make ready Your arrows on Your string towards their faces."

Psalm 21:11-12 (NKJV)

All that to say, it's okay to enjoy the blessing of the Lord. "... and He adds no sorrow to it." He will defend us. I can rejoice. And that's okay.

It's okay to have good things happen to and for you, regardless of how deserving you feel. Every good and perfect gift comes from GOD Himself. And if the Lord has something for me, I will receive it joyfully, like a kid at Christmas.

The title in the bible app of this scripture is "The Joy of Salvation." How true. My joy. I'm reminding myself to relax already.

Chapter 9

Fully Forgiven, Fully Forgive:

A Right Response

I was just woken up by a dream that I guess, in the best description I can give, disturbed me. I was with my husband, Ben, and two of his close friends. We were having some conversation about history. One of them said he knew Amerigo Vespucci, the guy who discovered America.

I said, "Dude, he's dead." So, he pulled his phone out and contacted him, and he showed me the screen, and it was him, but then I looked again after he faced the phone towards himself, I saw again, and it was a demon. I yelled out "BEN!!! ITS A DEMON!!!" They saw who the demon was pretending to be, but I saw what it was. Ben stood there for a minute, like in between, deciding who to believe because he trusted what I said I saw.

Then I woke up. I heard this humming in our house, and it scared me a little. So, I got up and went to see what was making the noise. My son, David, had music on. That was the humming I heard. I came back into my room and turned worship music on. Honestly, I was still a little shaken by the dream and asked Ben to hold me when I laid back down, but I couldn't stop thinking about this.

I was thinking, you know, I've been praying for my husband for years, and I have noticed my own prayer life change. I've declared scripture over him, thought I'd given him over to the Lord, let him go, or said I did. But one thing I learned and am still learning is this: I am not responsible for his spiritual walk. I'm responsible for my own.

God uses marriage to teach me how to love and respond like He would. When I started praying scripture over my husband, what happened is I began to see the potential God had placed in him, and when he would do things that I thought "didn't line up" with his GOD-GIVEN potential, I would get so discouraged about it and became angry at Ben. Like God, I'm declaring YOUR word over him; why is he still doing this or that? He continued to do things I thought were unreasonable and inappropriate for a Christian man. I judged him by my standards, which only invited discouragement and discontentment. This attitude never helped my husband to become the man of God he was meant to be. It wasn't until I gave up on having ANYTHING to do with his conversion that God really moved. I had to COMPLETELY release him to God and trust God to move.

I'm realizing something even more, even as I write. Ben is an amazing, AMAZING man, so good to us and his family, and he is a blessing from God, and I know that is true. But he belongs to God, and it's God's work in his life that will grow him.

Judging our husband's spiritual walk is a trap I think too many wives fall into; we think it's our responsibility. A friend triggered this realization in a prayer she prayed. We don't always see the clear picture right away. Even when we KNOW that God is working and can even see His response to our prayers, sometimes it's not fully manifested when we first look at it.

But the complete picture will be clear soon. God's full restoration is coming!

The deception out there is very real and very pointedly attacking men of God, especially fathers and husbands. I was seeing what the demon really was. It was pretending to be this person offering some "special relationship" to his friend.

The enemy is determined to destroy the family because he hates it. Deception is the tool he uses. He knows if he can destroy marriage, he can destroy family.

Picture the Trinity. The wife is a picture of the Holy Spirit in the home. We are not the Judge but an example of the Holy Spirit. How does the Holy Spirit respond to us when we are making mistakes, bad decisions, being unreasonable, or doing anything that leads away from Jesus?

It's not in judgment. It's in a spirit of gentleness, a sweet invitation to come wrap up in His arms and be restored to right standing with the Father. Conviction from the Father should be welcomed as an invitation for restoration.

The last thing I want to do when Ben and I are fighting is to say, "Babe, come love me, and let's be restored," but maybe that's the only thing I ever needed to do.

Yes, I will continue to pray for my husband, and will I mouth off again? Maybe. But I bet I'll think twice, knowing there is this very real deception in place to destroy him and me and everything God created our marriage to be.

I was praying and praying, and when I saw him still in a certain place, I thought it meant that God didn't answer my prayer. But God always answers prayer. In the most wonderful way possible. His. NOT MINE. Thank God.

I should never have been looking for my prayers answered in my husband, especially not his personal spiritual walk. That is between him and God. I should have always been looking to God, period.

"SOW FOR YOURSELF RIGHTEOUSNESS, reap mercy. Break up the fallow ground for it is time to seek the Lord TILL He comes and rains righteousness on you." (Hosea 10:12) NKJV

Whose righteousness? My own, not my husband's!

Do you know what fallow ground is? It is purposefully unsown ground. Farmers intentionally left ground unsown to limit production and restore fertility to the soil.

God said it was time to break up the fallow ground. It's time for production and life to come to this soil! It's time for fertility and life! Every single encounter I have in any relationship, especially in close relationships like my spouse, is an opportunity to learn more about Jesus and become closer to Him.

Though I don't get to make his decisions for him, I do get to make that decision. I do get to choose how I respond to him.

*Read this whole chapter! It's so good.

> "Do not lie to one another, since you have put off the old man with his deeds and have put on the new man who is renewed in knowledge according to the image of Him who created him where there is neither Greek, nor Jew, circumcised nor uncircumcised, barbarian, Scythian, slave nor free, but Christ is all and in all. Therefore, as the elect of God, holy and beloved, put on the tender mercies, kindness, humility, meekness, longsuffering; bearing with one another, and forgiving one another, if anyone has a complaint against another, even as Christ forgave you, so you also must do."

Colossians 3:9-13 (NKJV)

There is a level of forgiveness we offer each other that is a lie. When something happens in your marriage that upsets you, if your first response is anger that triggers a list of past mistakes your husband did that add to the flame, then there was never forgiveness there. There was just a "moving past it," or a "let's just tuck this away for later. I won't be mad about it now, but when the time comes, I'll pull it out, and it will become my dart." While it's tucked away in our hearts, it becomes like a rough leather, protecting the heart from being hurt again. When the heart is torn at the next injury, there the darts come flying. This creates more calluses and injury to our spouse, and guess what? The cycle continues.

FORGIVE, even as Christ FORGAVE YOU.

How does someone, any human, even do that?

The Lord's prayer:

"Forgive our trespasses, as we forgive those who have trespassed against us."

Matthew 6:12 (NMB)

"Then Peter came to Him and said, Lord how often shall my brother sin against me, and I forgive him? Up to seven times? Jesus said to him, I do not say to you up to seven times, but up to seventy times seven."

Matthew 18:21-22 (NKJV)

In a marriage, you will go through things. In any relationship for that matter. On the journey of "two becoming one," we end up hurting each other. Years and years of being hurt repeatedly without forgiving the right way can breed cold bitterness, discontentment, lack of respect, dishonor, etc. The opportunities to extend forgiveness are not few.

I honestly believe that because I allowed these injuries to remain unhealed inside of me for so long, this allowed the breeding ground for this disease to enter in. I didn't intentionally invite the disease, but by allowing the internal damage from unforgiveness, bitterness, and resentment to remain unhealed, this opened the door. As I navigate it, the Lord reveals His heart for healing to me and one by one, He is making me whole and teaching me as we walk this out together.

Is total forgiveness letting someone walk all over you?

Jesus fully forgave me, and I DARE NOT walk all over HIM. It's not even a consideration. It's an illogical thought, even. It's impossible to do. No one can take advantage of Jesus in that way. He is all powerful, sovereign God. I am only His creation, and so is my husband. Jesus said forgive each other as I have forgiven you.

How does Jesus forgive me?

Completely, utterly, and without regard to merit. When I mess up, He doesn't go back down the list of things I ever did and bring them up to make sure I'm still sorry I did those things before He offered me forgiveness.

Does that mean I have a right to withhold forgiveness if someone is unrepentant for the hurt they've caused me? That I can become angry, bitter, and cold? Don't we have to be sorry for our sins before God will restore us to right standing with Him? I always thought, YES, they NEED to be sorry. They are the ones who hurt me. But guess who was deceived there? ME!

Here's how Jesus responds when someone is going the wrong way:

> "What do you think, if a man has a hundred sheep, and one of them goes astray, does he not leave the ninety-nine and go the mountains to seek the one that is straying."

Matthew 18:12 (NKJV)

When we need restoration, GOD PURSUES US!

THANK GOD! Lord, thank you for every merciful grace you show us. Your mercies are NEW EACH DAY. Lord! We wake up daily to renewed mercy given to us by our heavenly Father.

That's the right response.

Chapter 10

Called and Chosen

How can God be anything other than GOOD? There is only one good, God.

The other day, I was reading Revelation and saw a scripture I had heard quoted many, many times.

> "These will make war with the Lamb, and the Lamb will
> overcome them, for He is the Lord of lords and King
> of kings; AND THOSE WHO ARE WITH HIM ARE
> CALLED, CHOSEN, AND FAITHFUL."
>
> Revelation 17:14 (NKJV)

I remember hearing "called, chosen, and faithful." I always heard that as "called – chosen and faithful." But I missed the comma after called. We are called, AND we are chosen, AND we are faithful. We should be—we, who are with Him. "Called and chosen" has stuck with me bouncing around in my head this week.

So, I have been thinking more and more about unbelievers and unbelief in general. Is anyone truly lost? Are there any lost causes? 1 John 17:12 says no, & 1 Peter 3:9 says, "He is not willing that any should perish."

So why is there unbelief? Why are there so many unbelievers?

I think the world is seeking the truth, but what happens when they encounter it? What truth do they seek, a truth, any truth?

I believe there is only One Truth: Jesus.

So, I've been praying for some friends who are not believing right now. I pray that God and the Holy Spirit will encounter them in an undeniable, inexplicable way. I still do pray this for them and even over myself and my family that we have undeniable Holy Spirit encounters because in times when the enemy comes with his lies, and he will, I can remember times when there are no explanations for the encounters I've had other than God's mercy, grace, miraculous intervention and involvement, and it shuts him up every time.

In 2008, my husband was in a bad motorcycle accident. He landed headfirst on pavement while not wearing a helmet. I found him in the street near our house, unconscious in a puddle of his own blood. Ambulances rushed him to a trauma center, and I followed behind. The doctors said he suffered a subdural hematoma, had inhaled blood and vomit into his lungs, and told me they were doing everything they could, but I should call our family to come. I reached out to our pastors at the time who came and prayed over him. In four days' time, he was awake, healed, and ready to go home!

Another time, I heard "How dare you come in here?" in my spirit when a demon tried to come into our sanctuary. As soon as I heard, "How dare you come in here?" I turned around, and it started manifesting. The woman fell to the ground, shrieking in a way I can only describe as "not human." Another time, I was driving on a slick road, and I lost control of my truck. I called out to God, "My God, save me!" I landed safely on a creek bank, though the water had risen and was rushing underneath the truck, now cradled between both ends of the creek bed.

I experienced these encounters myself. I saw this with my own eyes and heard this with my ears. I cannot be talked out of these personal encounters because they happened before my own eyes. So yes, I pray that they would have encounters with His Holy Spirit, too.

One thing I know is that you can't talk someone out of something they have personally experienced. So, I pray that God encounters them.

But is this why I believe in Him?

I was reading about the blind man Jesus healed on the sabbath in John 9. He said of Him (because the Jews were accusing Him):

"Whether this man is a sinner or not, I do not know, one thing I know: that though I was blind, now I see."

John 9:25 (NKJV)

The Jews couldn't understand Jesus and, therefore, wouldn't accept Him. Everything Jesus was did not align with their expectations, but when He was working miracles that they should believe in Him, they searched for reasons to accuse Him.

We should expect to be awed by Jesus and what He does, but it shouldn't surprise us because that is who He is! We should be in awe of Him, but we should also EXPECT Him to be WHO HE IS, Supernatural, miracle-working GOD, working through His people (us).

They were offended by Jesus because He didn't fit their mold. But Thank GOD! He works outside of our limits! It doesn't have to look like anything we've ever seen before.

Oh, please don't wait to understand before you believe. Faith comes first.

Read the word. If you are a truth seeker, open the word, ask Jesus, "Lord, open Your word to me," and watch Him do it. He came, not to condemn the world but to save it and to give us an amazing, abundantly fulfilled life.

They asked about the man who was born blind, 'Who sinned, this man or his parents that he was born blind?" Jesus said, "Neither this man nor his parents sinned, but that the works of God should be revealed in him." (John 9:3, NKJV)

We can have things happen to us that we did nothing to cause, but God will use those things to glorify His name and draw men unto Himself. We are called, and we are CHOSEN. The blind man was CHOSEN from birth! He was born blind, and the blindness he had lived with all his life was setting him up to meet JESUS so God would use him to reveal HIS work to the world. I can't even put words to this, the whole impact all this has. There is so much here. The man was a blind beggar, blind from birth. What purpose do you think people saw when they passed by him?

"Is this not he who sat and begged?" they said of him. I feel so sad at the purpose left sitting on the sidelines or miracles waiting to happen that we walk by because they don't look like whatever we deem qualifies, or it doesn't fit in what we expected it to look like.

There is so much God-given talent that God wants to be used so the world will know Him. So much potential and influence are there, but we don't submit, we don't let God use us, and we don't stop and listen. We are blind to what He wants to do because we can't understand what He's doing. All I know is I NEED Jesus. I NEED Him—every day. I need Him, and I know this. I still struggle to sit down and pray, and the enemy still tries to steal my faith.

Our enemy is so specifically cruel. He uses, just like with Job, things specifically curated to kill, steal, and destroy you. I mentioned earlier that I felt like with this disease, everything I identified with was attacked. But specifically, my faith. The enemy tells me, "You must not have faith to believe. If you had faith to believe, you would be healed. God must not even be real. If He were real, He would heal you. God must not care about your pain. If he cared about your pain, He would help you." He tells me I am alone because no one understands my pain. He says to me, I have no hope for healing because God is not going to heal me. Is God even real?

I must submit my thoughts and heart to Him daily.

"And you shall love the LORD your God with all your heart and with all your soul and with all your mind and with all your strength." (Ref: Deut. 6:5, Deut. 10:12, & Matthew 22:37, NKJV)

I must immerse myself in His truth to drown out the devil's lies. When I am consumed with His presence and truth, the enemy is the one with no hope!

Psalm 139:2-4 says, "You know my sitting down and my rising up. You understand my thought afar off. You comprehend my path and my lying down and are acquainted with all my ways. For there is not a word on my tongue, but behold you know it altogether." (NKJV)

What can I say to Him that He does not know? He knows every flaw. But HE draws me still. Because He is good, and He loves me. I must respond. I must come to Him. I am drawn unto Him.

But I believed in Him first by faith, not because I saw works but because I heard His word and believed Him. Because He is gracious, He called me. He says to marvel more at our names being written in the Book of Life rather than any manifestation we see here.

"Truly, truly, I say to you, he who does not enter the sheepfold by the door but climbs in by another way, that man is a thief and a robber. ² But he who enters by the door is the shepherd of the sheep. To him the gatekeeper opens. The sheep hear his voice, and he calls his own sheep by name and leads them out. When he has brought out all his own, he goes before them, and the sheep follow him, for they know his voice. A stranger they will not follow, but they will flee from him, for they do not know the voice of strangers." This figure of speech Jesus used with them, but they did not understand what he was saying to them. So Jesus again said to them, "Truly, truly, I say to you, I am the door of the sheep. All who came before me are thieves and robbers, but the sheep did not listen to them. I am the door. If anyone enters by me, he will be saved and will go in and out and find pasture. The thief comes only to steal and kill and destroy. I came that they may have life and have it abundantly. ¹¹ I am the good shepherd. The good shepherd lays down his life for the sheep. He who is a hired hand and not a shepherd, who does not own the sheep, sees the wolf coming and leaves the sheep and flees, and the wolf snatches them and scatters them. He flees because he is a hired hand and cares nothing for the sheep. I am the good shepherd. I know my own and my own know me, just as the Father knows me and I know the Father; and I lay down my life for the sheep. And I have other sheep that are not of this fold. I must bring them also, and they will listen to my voice. So there will be one flock, one shepherd. For this reason the Father loves me, because I lay down my life that I may take it up again. No one takes it from me, but I lay it down of my own accord. I have authority to lay it down, and I have authority to take it up again. This charge I have received from my Father."

John 10:1-18 (ESV)

He is the way!

> "I am the Good Shepherd, and I know My sheep, and am know by My own."

John 15 :14 (NKJV)

We are called, and we are chosen.

I was reminded when I read that "He goes before us" of a Psalm.

> "You have hedged me behind and before and You lay Your hand upon me."

Psalm 139:5 (NKJV)

If I hear Him and ignore the call, what can I say to the things that come against me? But if I listen to Him and I respond to His call with submission, and I follow Him, "I accept Your invitation, Father, I believe in You and Your works, I believe You sent Jesus Christ into the world to save us, I believe He died on the cross for my sin, and I believe that You love me with a perfect, unchangeable love." If I hear His call and I respond by following Him, the word says He is a hedge about me and surrounds me. I am protected. I am safe from anything this world has against me.

This world has nothing to offer and can do nothing to me or for me. This world is nothing. God is everything. He said He would send us the Holy Spirit to fulfill our joy. Fullness is found in the Father and the joy He offers.

If you are reading this, listen to the Call of the Father. He is calling YOU. He has chosen you!

He is not willing that anyone should perish but that all should come to repentance.

Repent? Repent of what?

We have all sinned and fallen short of the glory of God. I think we misunderstand His invitation. It's not to impose restrictions on us that we live in bondage to some invisible God.

It's to share with us His truth, THE truth. The TRUTH that gives us real freedom and that shows us real love- His love.

In the encounter with the blind man in John, He wanted to save the Jews. He pleaded with them, in John 10:37-38, "If you don't believe Me, believe the works." He told them that the scriptures testified of Himself. They WOULD NOT see it because it inconvenienced their way of life and traditions. They couldn't understand how He could be who He said He was because He wasn't what they expected.

I'm thinking about this virus going around today and the world; it's like the world wants to be in fear and is seeking to find things to worry about. But why? We don't understand. God is LOVE. God is truth. His truth is Jesus Christ, who came to take away the sins of the world. He arrived to give us truth, freedom, and abundant life, not a mediocre life. God doesn't do mediocre. He is above all!

This has been on my heart for a while, so I'll share it here. Now is the time to live in an expectation of blessing. I don't care what is happening outside. I know that God is moving. I am HIS. I belong to HIM. I chose to make Him my Lord and my King. I submit to Him. So, guess what that means? I can walk out my life NOW during this craziness in an expectation of blessing and expecting to be awed by Him.

Deuteronomy 28 says this:

28 "Now it shall come to pass, if you diligently obey the voice of the Lord your God, to observe carefully all His commandments which I command you today, that the Lord your God will set you high above all nations of the earth. ² And all these blessings shall come upon you and overtake you, because you obey the voice of the Lord your God: ³ "Blessed shall you be in the city and blessed shall you be in the country. 4. "Blessed shall

be the [a]fruit of your body, the produce of your ground and the increase of your herds, the increase of your cattle and the offspring of your flocks. ⁵ "Blessed shall be your basket and your kneading bowl. ⁶ "Blessed shall you be when you come in and blessed shall you be when you go out. ⁷ "The Lord will cause your enemies who rise against you to be defeated before your face; they shall come out against you one way and flee before you seven ways. ⁸ "The Lord will command the blessing on you in your storehouses and in all to which you set your hand, and He will bless you in the land which the Lord your God is giving you. ⁹The Lord will establish you as a holy people to Himself, just as He has sworn to you, if you keep the commandments of the Lord your God and walk in His ways. ¹⁰ Then all peoples of the earth shall see that you are called by the name of the Lord, and they shall be afraid of you. ¹¹ And the Lord will grant you plenty of goods, in the fruit of your body, in the increase of your livestock, and in the produce of your ground, in the land of which the Lord [b]swore to your fathers to give you. ¹² The Lord will open to you His good [c]treasure, the heavens, to give the rain to your land in its season, and to bless all the work of your hand. You shall lend to many nations, but you shall not borrow. ¹³ And the Lord will make you the head and not the tail; you shall be above only, and not be beneath, if you [d] heed the commandments of the Lord your God, which I command you today, and are careful to observe them. ¹⁴ So you shall not turn aside from any of the words which I command you this day, to the right or the left, to go after other gods to serve them." (NKJV)

I believe He wants to encounter us. He wants us all to see Him and what He does on earth. He desires to USE us to draw men unto Himself. I believe we can live in this expectation of blessing during any plague, crisis, or storm because my God walks on the waves. He quiets the storm. He brings water from the rock. He births a new thing. He thinks good thoughts towards us. He delivers us from every evil. He offers us the Bread of Life. He prepares a place for us in heaven and shelters us here on earth. He is our rest, our hope, our peace. He is good only always! Thank you, Jesus. We are called. We are chosen, and I will be faithful, Lord!

There's an old song that says, "I have read the end of the book, and we win!" Amen.

Don't say, "Not me." This is for YOU!

"Whoever Desires, let him take the water of life freely."
Revelation 22:17 (NKJV)

"Blessed are those who do His commandments that they may have the right to the tree of life and may enter through the gates into the city."
Revelation 22:14 (NKJV)

"I am the door, if anyone enters by Me, he will be saved and will go in and out and find pasture."
John 10:9 (NKJV)

Chapter 11

Wisdom and the Scoffer

The other day, I had a dream. There were two birds, one blackbird and one redbird. The birds flew into this fire inside a grill and died. A vulture came and tried to get to the birds that had perished in the fire, but it couldn't because the grill covered the coals. The vulture tried to get them but ended up burning his chest as he was trying to eat them. I wrote the dream down, wondered what it meant, and asked the Lord, and then just went about the day.

This morning I was reading 2 Peter 3: 1-8 which says "Beloved, I now write to you this second epistle (in both of which I stir up your pure minds by way of reminder), 2 that you may be mindful of the words which were spoken before by the holy prophets, and of the commandment of us, the apostles of the Lord and Savior, 3 knowing this first: that scoffers will come in the last days, walking according to their own lusts, 4 and saying, "Where is the promise of His coming? For since the fathers fell asleep, all things continue as they were from the beginning of creation." 5 For this they willfully forget: that by the word of God the heavens were of old, and the earth standing out of water and in the water, 6 by which the world that then existed perished, being flooded with water. 7 But the heavens and the earth which are now preserved by the same word, are reserved for fire until the day of judgment and perdition of ungodly men. 8 But, beloved, do not forget this one thing, that with the Lord one day is as a thousand years, and a thousand years as one day. (NKJV)

I heard about a study that found that the universe was held together by soundwaves. When I heard of it, I thought it was interesting, but I wasn't surprised because in Genesis, the bible says, God spoke, and He created. It just sounded to me like science was catching up to the bible, so I didn't read any further into the studies.

But after reading this scripture, I looked up the studies just because God reminded me of them, and I found some interesting facts. Still, one of the common threads written in these studies that I looked into was that they can prove that matter can be created from sound. Measurable matter can be created from sound waves. Come on now! I love it. Google it! Lots of resources are available for you if you dig a little.

When this was written, it was the month of April, or in the Hebrew calendar, the first month of the new year; also, we were in "the year of the mouth."

I feel like we have a choice of the sounds we let ourselves listen to and a choice as to what we speak and what is created in our atmospheres.

2 Peter was warning us about the scoffer, the mocker, the false prophet, and the false teacher. (I looked up the definition of scoffer, and all these terms were pulled up). How rightly Peter refers to Balaam, who, by trickery, brought corruption to the house of Israel because he sought after riches and the king's favor.

> He warns, "These are wells without water clouds carried by a tempest, for whom is reserved the blackness of darkness forever. For when they speak great swelling of words of emptiness, they allure through the lust of the flesh through lewdness, the ones who have actually escaped from those who live in error. While they promised them liberty, they themselves are slaves of corruption for by whom a person is overcome, by him he is brought into bondage."

> 2 Peter 2:17-18 (NKJV)

There is a common theme in the bible about the power of the tongue and the power of the spoken word, starting in Genesis when God spoke and created the universe. In Numbers, when God wanted to reveal His glory by bringing water out of the rock the second time, He told Moses to SPEAK to the Rock. He struck the rock and missed out on his full blessing, but God wanted him to speak to it. (Numbers 20:7) What would have happened if Moses had spoken to the rock then?

> "A man's stomach shall be satisfied from the fruit of his mouth; from the produce of his lips he shall be filled. Death and life are in the power of the tongue, and those who love it will eat its fruit."

Proverbs 18:20-21 (NKJV)

> "A man shall eat by the fruit of his mouth..." Proverbs 13:2 (NKJV)

> "A man will be satisfied with good from the fruit of his mouth."

Proverbs 12:14 (NKJV)

So, what about the Scoffer? What does a scoffer do?

The scoffer mocks. He is a mocker.

The scoffer hates wisdom. He is prideful and arrogant. It does no good to argue with him or try to rebuke him.

A scoffer is the spirit of the narcissist, pride, and Jezebel in the worst combination.

Sidebar – Narcissism: The problem with dealing with the narcissist is they will never apologize. In his/her mind, they have done nothing wrong.

This person will convince themselves that anything they have done was not harmful, since in their mind the benefit to themselves outweighed any potential danger to the victim. The damage to the victim was likely never considered. They will always be their own first priority and never recognize the harm they have caused despite the blatant selfishness of their actions. This person will always be the innocent victim. They will never accept any responsibility of wrongdoing, therefore any fake apology they muster will only be after they have been caught doing something harmful; even then, they will consider themselves the victim and look for someone else to blame, usually a gas-lit victim so conditioned to their environment, they don't even realize what is happening. The narcissist will be wholly convinced of their being right under every circumstance. You will not win an argument with this person. You will only suspend it for it appear again later as twisted fuel. This person will not change without deliverance from the Holy Spirit. They will not be able to do this on their own.

A set boundary will cause this person to throw a fit, but it's the only option. This person is not safe. Guard your peace. Cut them off.

The Pharisaical Narcissist claims to love God but is far from Him. This person twists the word of God to fit their narrative. The love of Christ is not in them. They will always be their own first priority.

Until true deliverance happens, you cannot be safe with this person.

A note to the spouses who stay in unsafe or abusive relationships because you believe the bible says you have to; it DOES NOT. It says you can leave unto the Lord. Not leave and go and get remarried. I am not suggesting divorce. I'm saying if you are in danger and experiencing abuse of any kind, go to safety, even if that means away from your spouse.

The proper response to the scoffer is to cast out the spirit of the scoffer. How? Humility.

Peter said, "They speak evil of things they do not understand."

A scoffer will ask why God allowed this, and if He can do something about it, why doesn't he do something about it?

"Where is God in the middle of all this, and if God loves you, then … (fill in the blank)?"

The spirit of the scoffer was present at the crucifixion of Jesus when they mocked Him, saying, "If you are who you say you are, call down angels, come down off that cross," etc.

If God loves me, how can He not let me see His manifested glory on this earth? Wouldn't He want us to see that? Wouldn't He want to show that to us? How could He not let me live out each day, showing Himself available and ready to answer our needs while we're here living on earth? The bible also says that:

"It is our Father's good pleasure to give us the Kingdom."

Luke 12:32 (NKJV)

"Seek the kingdom first and all these things will be added unto us."

Matthew 6:33 (NKJV)

"Therefore I say to you, do not worry about your life, what you will eat or what you will drink; nor about your body, what you will put on. Is not life more than food and the body more than clothing?"

Matthew 6:25 (NKJV)

The next scripture in 2 Peter 3:9 says that, "He's not slack concerning His promises to us as some count slackness, but He is long suffering toward us not willing that any should perish but that all should come to repentance." (NKJV)

This is why we live here in these times: He wants us all to repent.

What an opportunity we have now, during this time, to recognize the call of the Lord, who is speaking with His own mouth His answer.

What a time we have and what an opportunity we have right now to respond to this invitation from heaven that says, repent, come close to Me, and be intimate with Me; let Me wash away whatever it is. Let Me give you My wisdom and understanding.

Don't follow the way of the scoffer, don't follow the invitation of the mocker, don't envy them.

Proverbs 2:7-8 says, "He stores up sound wisdom for the upright; He is a shield to those who walk uprightly; He guards the paths of justice and preserves the way of His Saints." (NKJV)

"Incline your ear to wisdom, and apply your heart to understanding; yes, if you cry out for discernment, and lift up your voice for understanding, if you seek her as silver, and search for her as for hidden treasures, then you will understand the fear of the Lord, and find the knowledge of God. For the Lord gives wisdom; from His mouth come knowledge and understanding." Proverbs 2:2-6 (NKJV)

Proverbs 8:13-14 says, (this is wisdom speaking), "The fear of the Lord is to hate evil; Pride and arrogance and the evil way and the perverse mouth I hate. Council is mine, and sound wisdom; I am understanding, I have strength." (NKJV)

So, in wisdom, there is strength, understanding, and council.

Proverbs 2:10-15 says, "When wisdom enters your heart, and knowledge is pleasant to your soul, discretion will preserve you; understanding will keep you, to deliver you from the way of evil, from the man who speaks perverse things, from those who leave the paths of uprightness to walk in the ways of darkness; who rejoice in doing evil, and delight in the perversity of the wicked; whose ways are crooked, and who are devious in their paths;" (NKJV)

Who does that sound like? That scripture reminds me so much of the warning from Peter, how he's talking about them walking in their own ways and using lewdness and lust to deceive the people. "Scoffers will come in the last days, walking according to their lusts." So, can you see the deception there? Can you see Proverb's warning and Peter reminding us? So, God wants to give us wisdom.

Right now, I think it's important to recognize what God is wanting to do, to say, and to show us. We are to cry out for the wisdom and understanding He offers us. We're not to speak evil of things we don't understand, but we're to cry out for discernment and for His knowledge. This is how we will find our strength, because in the word of God there is joy, and in the wisdom of God there is strength.

> "Do not correct a scoffer lest he will hate you, rebuke a wise man and he will love you."
>
> Proverbs 9:8 (NKJV)

Our options are to follow wisdom or foolishness.

Why couldn't the scoffer receive correction?

When I started receiving revelation in the word, I would be so excited about the words I found and sharing them. I'd send them to my pastors or friends and say, "Look what the Lord showed me!!" They were very encouraging. Sometimes, I'd think, "Man, this word is for the whole church! I would want to get up on the platform and tell the whole church." Someone once said, "That's a good word for you!" I thought, "For me? This is a good word for everybody." I didn't understand how it wasn't to them a word that should be yelled from the pulpit. I understand now.

Any time we receive a word from God or revelation in the word, when He shows us something that could be a word for the whole church, it is always a personal word for yourself. It's always a personally applicable revelation that can apply to your life right now in your season.

When He gives me a word about anything, I want to see where it applies carefully. For example, in this word about wisdom and the scoffer, I need to ask about the condition of my soul. Are there areas in my life where I'm listening to the voice of foolishness, or the cry of the mocker, or doubting God, or being disobedient, disillusioned, or rebellious, or any of those things Peter describes of the scoffer? And if I am, I repent of them.

> "Folly is joy to him who is destitute of discernment but a man of understanding walks uprightly."
>
> Proverbs 15:21 (NKJV)

"A scoffer does not love one who corrects him, nor will he go to the wise…"

Proverbs 15:12 (NKJV)

"The mouth of him who has understanding seeks knowledge but the mouth of fools feeds on foolishness."
Proverbs 15:14 (NKJV)

"A wise son heeds his father's instruction, but a scoffer does not listen to rebuke."

Proverbs 13:1 (NKJV)

"The proud and haughty man "scoffer" is his name, he acts with arrogant pride."

Proverbs 21:24 (NKJV)

So why couldn't the scoffer receive correction?

Where there is no humility, there can be no repentance.

Remember the dream? I searched what the birds meant and what the vulture meant. I found one of the definitions of a vulture when talking about the words used in the Hebrew bible: the vulture could have also been an eagle. Also, the red bird could be a mockingbird.

This study was already fun for me, but when I saw this, it's now super fun.

I read Proverbs 30:17, "The eye that mocks his father and scorns obedience to his mother the ravens of the valley will pick it out and the young eagles will eat it." (NKJV)

What happens when your eye is plucked out? You become blind. You lose your vision and your perspective; you don't understand what's around you because you're blind.

Then, the dream started to make sense. I'm still chewing on what it means, but I'm awed by the imagery and how God is so creative in speaking to us.

Proverbs 29:1 says, "He who is often rebuked and hardens his neck will suddenly be destroyed and that without remedy." (NKJV)

There is a call for the sound of repentance right now.

And I feel like there is a warning here that if you've been rebuked and you harden your neck, you ignore wisdom, you reject wisdom, you're stuck in pride, you're blinded by arrogance and disobedience and following your way, it says:

"He who is often rebuked and hardens his neck, will suddenly be destroyed and that without remedy."

Proverbs 29:1 (NKJV)

That's a scary one. But I remember His promise, "God is not slack concerning His promise but long-suffering, not willing that any should perish, but that all should come to repentance."

2 Peter 3:9 (NKJV)

The invitation of repentance is here. There is a call for the sound of repentance right now.

"Cast out the scoffer and contention will leave you, yes strife and reproach will cease."

Proverbs 22:10 (NKJV)

Well, how? How do you cast out the spirit of the scoffer?

Since it's the spirit of pride, do it with humility and repentance. What brought about the restoration of Job was repentance and humility. Repentance when he heard God's answer, and humility when he prayed for his friends.

We must listen to the call we are given. There is a voice calling out right now that wants nothing more than to devour your faith and lead you into a life of destitution. It ultimately glorifies rebellion and disobedience. It proudly flaunts disrespect and arrogance.

But there is another voice calling, the voice of wisdom inviting you to search her out, to receive God's knowledge, discernment, and understanding—a promise of Godly wisdom that brings joy and strength and secures the right path.

It's the voice of God. It's the sound of wisdom.

Galatians 6:7 warns us, "Do not be deceived; God is not mocked, whatever a man sows, that he will reap." (NKJV) Proverbs tell us we will be satisfied by the fruit of our lips. So, what are your lips speaking? What are the sounds surrounding you?

"He is not slack concerning His promise but long-suffering, that all should come to repentance."

2 Peter 3:9 (NKJV)

If you're waiting on God to answer you and you are disillusioned or discouraged because you can't see what He is doing yet, don't give up hope. Wait on Him. Press into Him. Bind yourself, entwine yourself together with His promises.

Proverbs 23:17-18 says, "Do not let your heart envy sinners but be zealous for the fear of the Lord all the day for surely there is a hereafter, and your hope will not be cut off." (NKJV)

Proverbs 24:5 says, "A wise man is strong yes, a man of knowledge increases strength." (NKJV)

If you're in that place where you feel like you have no strength to endure, you can't go on; seek after wisdom. He stores up wisdom for us. A wise man increases strength. There is strength in wisdom.

Proverbs 24:10 says, "If you faint in the day of adversity, your strength is small."

Our strength doesn't have to be small because there is a promise of stored wisdom that can give us strength and increased knowledge. Seek after knowledge and wisdom. Watch the Lord give you strength. **57**

Chapter 12

What Are You Planting?

We can't sow manipulation, threats, or punishments and expect righteousness or any Godly fruit.

If our concern is for genuine repentance or for real transformation for a struggling brother or sister, then we won't take their iniquities personally. Instead, we will be moved with compassion for them. We will be moved to pray for their soul, that it becomes one with Jesus because we seek their wholeness and their fulfillment.

Yes, it's heartbreaking to see the ones we love fall and struggle, but why do we think we must punish them? Please stop. There can be no reconciliation if you sow manipulation, judgment, discord, wrath, and abuse.

The bible says sow peace reap righteousness. "Now the fruit of righteousness is sown in peace by those who make peace." (James 3:18, NKJV)

Even writing this, I have to examine my own heart. Am I angry at the self-righteousness that I think I see in people, and then am I now judging them, or do I genuinely want transformation for the lost and broken? That they be made whole and know the Love of Jesus? God help me. The bible also says sow righteousness and reap mercy. (Hosea 10:12, NKJV)

James 1:20 tells us, "That the wrath of man does not produce the righteousness of God." (NKJV)

Compassion must be our prayer. "Even as I have loved you" is our commandment. If the love of Christ is punishment, we'd all be in hell with no hope of reconciliation with Him. But the Love of Christ is anything but. It's hope, kindness, mercy, truth, compassion, and more.

Jesus prepares us in Matthew for a day where the love of many grows cold. He says that many will be offended and betray one another, and because lawlessness abounds, the love of many will grow cold. Lawlessness is when we take the law into our own hands and make ourselves judges of one another.

But the hope here is that the word will be preached to every nation.

"This Gospel" the word says. God, let us hear you. Help us to genuinely love and be concerned for one another.

As You have loved us, may we love one another, help us to sow peace.

Make us like You, Lord.

In Jesus' Name. Amen

Chapter 13

The Good Samaritan,

an Unexpected Perspective of Fragrant Worship

I saw something while reading Luke 10:30-37. It's the story of the good Samaritan.

> In reply Jesus said: "A man was going down from Jerusalem to Jericho, when he was attacked by robbers. They stripped him of his clothes, beat him and went away, leaving him half dead. A priest happened to be going down the same road, and when he saw the man, he passed by on the other side. So too, a Levite, when he came to the place and saw him, passed by on the other side. But a Samaritan, as he traveled, came where the man was; and when he saw him, he took pity on him. He went to him and bandaged his wounds, pouring on oil and wine. Then he put the man on his own donkey, brought him to an inn and took care of him. The next day he took out two denarii[a] and gave them to the innkeeper. 'Look after him,' he said, 'and when I return, I will reimburse you for any extra expense you may have.'" (NIV)

I've heard this story so many times, but God breathed a new light on it for me.

The scripture says, "A man went down from Jerusalem to Jericho." I thought, "You know, Lord, You never say anything just to be saying it." So, I felt it has to be specific. Why was he going from Jerusalem to Jericho?

I looked up "Jerusalem." It, of course, means "the holy city." So, what is Jericho? I read something that said the word Jericho means "moon" and that the city was named after a moon god that was worshipped there. But it also could mean "fragrance."

This is cool. I think "Fragrant Worship."

Do you remember what happened at Jericho? I'm getting excited now as I am starting to understand. Do you recall how the city of Jericho was conquered?

Joshua 6:20 says, "So the people shouted when the priests blew the trumpets. And it happened when the people heard the sound of the trumpet, and the people shouted with a great shout, that the wall fell down flat. Then the people went up into the city, every man straight before him and they took the city." (NIV)

God said, "Worship is Mine!"

So, this man Jesus is talking about leaves Jerusalem and goes to Jericho.

Have you ever known someone who left the church to do something or left a job or situation you'd known them in, and you thought, "Hmmm, I just don't think that's right," and maybe you judged them or disapproved, and your disapproval showed? Or perhaps you just heard about it but didn't say anything but thought, "Yeah, that's probably not right for them." A new job, a relationship, a move, or just time away, who knows why they left the situation? And then, something happens to them that hurts them on their journey away. Your temptation is to say or think, "See, I knew this would happen to them."

Jesus was telling us about how thieves met this man, and they beat him, stripped him, and left him half dead. The man sees the pastor pass by and do nothing. What do you think he thought to himself? Then he sees the Levite come near him, look at him, and pass by. I wonder what the injured man thought to himself.

The Levite represents the church. The priest can represent a pastor or someone in a high position that maybe you respect or look up to. Then, a Samaritan.

Do you know what the word Samaritan means?

It means guardians, watchers, keepers/defenders of the Torah/law. I thought that was interesting. But remember, Samaritans in Jesus' time weren't allowed to worship with the Jews. This is interesting. This Samaritan saw the man, and Jesus said he had compassion for him.

> "But a certain Samaritan, as he journeyed, came to where he was and when he saw him, he bandaged his wounds, pouring on oil and wine." Luke 10:30-34 (NKJV)

This reminded me of the Holy Spirit who is also called the Comforter.

This also represents the blood of Jesus, or mercy.

> "…and he set him on his own animal brought him to an inn and took care of him. On the next day when he departed, took out two denarii, gave them to the inn keeper and said to him "Take care of him and whatever more you spend when I come again, I will repay you."
>
> Luke 10:34-35 (NKJV)

This Samaritan was even willing to pay this man's debt!

Jesus asked the lawyer (I also think it's interesting that He was talking to a lawyer because, remember, Samaritan means defender of the law),

> "Which of these do you think was a neighbor to him who fell among thieves, and he said, "he who showed mercy."
>
> Luke 10:36-37 (NKJV)

The bible says the lawyer, wanting to justify himself, asked,

"Well, who is my neighbor?"

Luke 10:29 (NKJV)

I was just thinking about this man and how he was going somewhere, and he found himself injured, beaten, and left for dead. This experience alone must have been traumatizing, but when he saw the priest pass by and do nothing, then he saw the other "man of God" pass by, even come near him, LOOK at him, and walk off.

Were they thinking,

"That's what he gets for leaving Jerusalem,"

"See, pride comes before a fall,"

"He should have never been going to Jericho anyway."

"I knew this would happen; that is what he gets."

I don't know, but the Samaritan came and showed him mercy and compassion. The familiar community that the man had seen in Jerusalem let him down, and God used a Samaritan to show the love, mercy, kindness, and compassion of the Holy Spirit.

We must be careful not to judge someone's journey. We don't know what God is doing in them.

I'm sure he thought these two people in those places would surely stop and help him because he wasn't dead; he was left for dead, he was half dead, but he wasn't dead, and he needed help. I wonder if he saw them passing by, and when he saw those people pass him by, people, who maybe he had expected more from, just passed him by, and even one came, looked at him, saw him, and walked away; I wonder what he thought, I wonder how he felt.

Well, there's a lot here, but I want to say this: just because someone has a certain position doesn't mean that they will live up to your expectations of them in that position.

We must find our complete satisfaction and fullness in Jesus alone. He is it. The only way. The only truth, the only life. Its Him.

Nothing and no one will ever be enough. It's only Jesus. So, when people disappoint you, remember Judas had a high position, too, but it didn't make him Jesus. There is only ONE.

Then the Samaritan came, and he showed him mercy and kindness. He took time to bandage his wounds, to show and share the comfort of the Holy Spirit, and to share God's mercy and grace. A Samaritan did that.

He used what he had. He put him on his animal. He had to walk the animal, put the man on top, and then lead him to the inn. The Samaritan went out of his way to care for this stranger—this guy from Jerusalem, whom the Samaritan wasn't even allowed to worship with.

We go through things; we try to make the best decisions for ourselves. If you're a Christian, you should always submit your day to the Lord, your life, and everything to Him because He promises to lead, guide, and direct our paths. So, I always pray about everything.

God, the Holy Spirit can speak to us, direct us, and do anything inside of us He wants to. Sometimes we will make decisions for ourselves that others disagree with. That's okay. They don't have to agree with them.

When you see somebody making a decision you disagree with, you can be neighborly to that person, merciful and compassionate. Be their God friend, and love your neighbor.

"Who is your neighbor?"

This injured man, who walked away from the holy city, who maybe made a wrong decision, was left injured on the road.

"Who is your neighbor?"

Your neighbor isn't everyone who agrees with you or lives or makes decisions how you think they should.

These thieves attacked him, stole his clothes and left him for dead. If something happens to a brother or sister, where they find themselves stripped, beaten, and traumatized by some event they encountered on their journey, we have an opportunity to be kind, gracious, merciful and to share the Holy Spirit. We can pour the oil and wine of the Holy Spirit on their wounds, not condemnation and judgment.

As Christians, we should be careful when our brothers and sisters are walking through different seasons or situations in their lives. If you know, they hear the Holy Spirit, especially those that we know that they hear from Him; if they're doing something that you (in your opinion) disagree with, guess what, honey, that's none of your business. You know you can pray for them, but don't share your judgment; don't share condemnation and ridicule.

Share the Holy Spirit, share the oil, and share the wine.

Going through these journeys, we must never underestimate the fragrant worship that can come out of them and the reach that can happen in the world when God brings us out of them.

I wonder how grateful this man from Jerusalem was after his life had been spared, and I wonder what new perspective he had after being shown kindness and compassion by a Samaritan. I wonder what fragrance his redeemed worship brought to heaven.

Hearing from the Holy Spirit?

Yes, He speaks to us! This is available to any Christian. Just ask the Lord, and He will speak. He is always speaking. Ask the Lord to open the scriptures to you.

Read the story of John the Baptist when, in Elizabeth's womb, filled with the Holy Spirit, jumped for joy when Mary, pregnant with Jesus, entered the room.

"When Elizabeth heard Mary's greeting, the baby leaped in her womb, and Elizabeth was filled with the Holy Spirit. In a loud voice she exclaimed: "Blessed are you among women, and blessed is the child you will bear! But why am I so favored, that the mother of my Lord should come to me?

As soon as the sound of your greeting reached my ears, the baby in my womb leaped for joy."

Luke 1:41-44 (NKJV)

Read the story in Acts 2 when tongues of fire rested on the heads of the 120, and they all spoke in various tongues:

"And suddenly there came a sound from heaven, as of a rushing mighty wind, and it filled the whole house where they were sitting. [3] Then there appeared to them [a] divided tongues, as of fire, and one sat upon each of them. [4] And they were all filled with the Holy Spirit and began to speak with other tongues, as the Spirit gave them utterance." (NKJV)

Read Acts 10:44 when Peter began to understand that the Holy Spirit was for everyone:

"While Peter was still speaking these words, the Holy Spirit fell upon all those who heard the word. And those of the circumcision who believed were astonished, as many as came with Peter, because the gift of the Holy Spirit had been poured out on the Gentiles also. For they heard them speak with tongues and magnify God." (NKJV)

Read Acts 19:1-5:

"And it happened, while Apollos was at Corinth, that Paul, having passed through the upper regions, came to Ephesus. And finding some disciples he said to them, "Did you receive the Holy Spirit when you believed?" So they said to him, "We have not so much as heard whether there is a Holy Spirit." And he said to them, "Into what then were you baptized?" So they said, "Into John's baptism. "Then Paul said, "John indeed baptized with a baptism of repentance, saying to the people that they should believe on Him who would come after him, that is, on Christ Jesus." When they heard this, they were baptized in the name of the Lord Jesus. And when Paul had laid hands on them, the Holy

Spirit came upon them, and they spoke with tongues and prophesied. Now the men were about twelve in all." (NKJV)

Read about John prophesying the coming of the Lord who would baptize us with Fire and the Holy Spirit in Mark 1:6:

"Now John was clothed with camel's hair and with a leather belt around his waist, and he ate locusts and wild honey. And he preached, saying, "There comes One after me who is mightier than I, whose sandal strap I am not worthy to stoop down and loose. I indeed baptized you with water, but He will baptize you with the Holy Spirit." (NKJV)

Read Romans 8:26 where we are admonished to pray in the Spirit:

"Likewise the Spirit also helps in our weaknesses. For we do not know what we should pray for as we ought, but the Spirit Himself makes intercession for us with groanings which cannot be uttered. Now He who searches the hearts knows what the mind of the Spirit is, because He makes intercession for the saints according to the will of God." (NKJV)

Read Jude 1:20-21:

"But you, beloved, building yourselves up on your most holy faith, praying in the Holy Spirit, keep yourselves in the love of God, looking for the mercy of our Lord Jesus Christ unto eternal life." (NKJV)

Read Ephesians 5:18:

And do not be drunk with wine, in which is dissipation; but be filled with the Spirit." (NKJV)

Read Luke 24:49:

"Behold, I send the Promise of My Father upon you; but tarry in the city [m]of Jerusalem until you are endued with power from on high." (NKJV)

Read again in Matthew 3:11:

"I indeed baptize you with water unto repentance, but He who is coming after me is mightier than I, whose sandals I am not worthy to carry. He will baptize you with the Holy Spirit and fire." (NKJV)

Read 1 Corinthians 14:1-25

" Pursue love, and desire spiritual gifts, but especially that you may prophesy[2] For he who speaks in a tongue does not speak to men but to God, for no one understands him; however, in the spirit he speaks mysteries. But he who prophesies speaks edification and exhortation and comfort to men. He who speaks in a tongue edifies himself, but he who prophesies edifies the church. I wish you all spoke with tongues, but even more that you prophesied; for he who prophesies is greater than he who speaks with tongues, unless indeed he interprets, that the church may receive edification. But now, brethren, if I come to you speaking with tongues, what shall I profit you unless I speak to you either by revelation, by knowledge, by prophesying, or by teaching? Even things without life, whether flute or harp, when they make a sound, unless they make a distinction in the sounds, how will it be known what is piped or played? For if the trumpet makes an uncertain sound, who will prepare for battle? So likewise you, unless you utter by the tongue words easy to understand, how will it be known what is spoken? For you will be speaking into the air. There are, it may be, so many kinds of languages in the world, and none of them is without significance. Therefore, if I do not know the meaning of the language, I shall be a foreigner to him who speaks, and he who speaks will be a foreigner to me.· Even so you, since you are zealous for spiritual gifts, let it be for the edification of the church that you seek to excel. Therefore let him who speaks in a tongue pray that he may interpret· For if I pray in a tongue, my spirit prays, but my understanding is unfruitful. What is the conclusion then? I will pray with the spirit, and I will also pray with the understanding. I will sing with the spirit, and I will also sing with the understanding. Otherwise, if you bless with the spirit, how will he who occupies the place of the uninformed say "Amen" at your giving of thanks, since he does not understand what you say? For you indeed give thanks well, but the other is not edified. I thank my God I speak with tongues more than you all; yet in the church I would rather speak five words with my understanding, that I may teach others also, than ten thousand words in a tongue. Brethren, do not be children in understanding; however, in malice be babes, but in understanding be mature. In the law it is written: "With men of other tongues and other lips I will speak to this people; And yet, for all that, they will not hear Me, "says the Lord. Therefore tongues are for a sign, not to those who believe but to unbelievers; but prophesying is not for unbelievers but for those who believe. Therefore if the whole church comes together in one place, and all speak with tongues, and there come in those who are uninformed or unbelievers, will they not say that you are [l]out of your mind? But if all prophesy, and an unbeliever or an uninformed person comes in, he is convinced by all, he is convicted by all. And thus the secrets of his heart are revealed; and so, falling down on his face, he will worship God and report that God is truly among you."

(NKJV)

God speaks and He teaches us with His Holy Spirit. This is for you! Don't wait to be filled with His presence. Life changes for the better when you allow the fullness of the Lord to come.

Chapter 14

The Right Side of the Cloud

John the Baptist said, "Bear fruits worthy of repentance," (Matthew 3:8, NKJV) and "Even now, "The ax is laid to the root of the trees." (Matthew 3:10, NKJV)

In the exodus, there was a defined moment when the Lord went behind the children whom He had called out of Egypt (the land of bondage) into the promised land. There was a defined moment in time where He went and stood behind them, and He was a cloud of darkness and confusion for their enemy, but He was a lighted path to His chosen ones!

This is our promise. Nahum tells us:

> "The LORD is slow to anger, and great in power, and will not at all acquit the wicked: the LORD hath His way in the whirlwind and in the storm, and the clouds are the dust of His feet."

> Nahum 1:3 (NKJV)

The clouds are the dust of His feet.

So, there's this battle for souls on Earth, and we find ourselves in the middle of it. The Church is the army.

Joshua told the children of Israel,

> "Now therefore, fear the Lord and serve Him in sincerity and in truth and put away the gods which your fathers served on the other side of the river (rebellion) and in Egypt (bondage). Serve the Lord! And if it seems evil to you to serve the Lord, choose for yourselves this day whom you

will serve... but as for me and my house we will serve the Lord."

Joshua 24:15 (NKJV)

Make a decision, but be sincere about your decision.

There's a moment when you will have to resolve in your heart WHO you will serve. Are you walking into the unknown with Jesus and trusting Him, or are you staying behind with the enemy? This is the choice. It MUST have been terrifying for the Israelites to step foot into the water, to leave a land they had called home for over 400 years.

They had asked for this, a deliverance, and God sent His answer. His deliverer. But they had to decide to go. They had to choose to step in the water.

I pray for the spirit of the initiator to come to this earth. It is said of Nahshon, a prince of the Jews, one of the appointed heads of the tribes after the numbering, that he stepped first into the Red Sea and was first to bring an offering to the Tabernacle of the Lord in the wilderness.

We need that initiator spirit in the earth today. We need the brave princes who will step first into the unknown. We need the Calebs, and Joshuas who will declare the victory. There's a moment in time coming where there will be line drawn behind God's people separating them from the oncoming enemy. The cloud He is in will be confusion and darkness for the enemy but light for His church.

Whose side are you on?

If you knew someone was sneaking around, lurking in any and every corner, looking for an opportunity to come in and hurt your children, destroy your home, steal everything you own, destroy your peace and your future, not only yours, but your children's as well, what would you do? I think you would be standing guard against that enemy, not just waiting for him to come in but aggressively snuffing out and eliminating the threat. You would do everything you could to prevent this attack.

I wonder if we think because he is a quiet enemy at times that, he isn't much of a threat. The problem is if you think he's quiet, you're not listening, and if you don't hear or see the attack coming, that alone should be concerning.

No, he's not a threat if you are on the right side.

His plan is obvious, and we have a clear warning and a battle strategy that we cannot lose. We lose when we try to change the battle plan or are on the wrong side.

Jack Graham said this in his book, *A Man of God*, "In Ephesians 6:18 Paul says that we need to be "watchful" in prayer. This term refers to a soldier watching at his post. We are to be at our prayer post as though we are in a battle because we are. We know that Satan is stalking our kids, but we can engage in effective and victorious spiritual combat for them through believing prayer, constantly persevering in the name of the Lord Jesus Christ."

"Watch and Pray" is also what Jesus says.

"Watch and pray, lest you enter into temptation. The spirit indeed is willing, but the flesh is weak."

Matthew 26:41 (NKJV)

This is it. Watch and pray. Jesus told us, "The spirit is indeed willing, but the flesh is weak." Our flesh is weak, so Paul says we have to die daily to it, its desires and tendencies. When you wake up in the morning, put into your mind a resolve to be on the right side of the cloud, have the mind of Christ, and want the things that He desires for you for that day.

The apparent lack of the fear of God in this earth is concerning to me. We are blatant with our disrespect. Do we recognize conviction anymore? It's why we are to put on a new man, one born of the spirit and not of the flesh.

Choose this day whose side you are on. There's a moment coming where the Lord will stand behind His church and the line will be drawn between His church and our enemy.

John was warning us,

> "Therefore, bear fruits worthy of repentance… And even
> now the ax is laid to the root of the trees."

Matthew 3:8-10 (NKJV)

Things are about to start falling here; we have to be repentant. Our hearts, the posture of our hearts, should bear fruit worthy of repentance and be sincere in our pursuit and approach to God.

An unrepentant, insincere heart is unwilling to admit its faults and reluctant to change. True strength is integrity, a willingness to admit fault and to be corrected.

In his book, Jack Graham says, "Weak churches and weak families are the results of weak leaders. We have popular preachers today, but not very many powerful ones. It's up to us to be strong in the faith." He reminds us, "The only way to make a truly lasting difference is to change hearts, and that happens one heart and one life at a time."

We have to admit when our hearts need repentance. Confess your sins, and repent. Are you unrepentant?

Well, ask yourself this. Do you look like the world? Is there a clear line in your heart and mind that separates you from looking like the world? Do you know what grieves Him, and does that grieve you? When was the last time you had an honest moment with God where you were truly convicted in your heart and desired Him to bring healing to your soul?

When believers look like the world, we render our testimony ineffective. The ax is laid at the trees; things are about to come out! You think you've gotten away with something, be reminded our God is an avenger and He is coming. He is responding to the cries of injustice.

It shouldn't be said of Christians that we're drunk, high, watching porn, have secret relationships, stealing, manipulative, selfishly motivated, pretentious liars. God says it's dissipation, in other words, blatant and outright waste. Please stop wasting away. The ax is laid at the trees. We pretend to be sanctified when our hearts have become numb to the voice of the Lord, and if we're not careful, we will miss the harvest!

The world is in need of a Savior. The One we profess to know and love. But do we? Why would the world want our God if we, ourselves don't even obey and there's no clear distinction between us and them? And why don't we obey? What is in the believers' heart that keeps him from submitting fully and surrendering entirely over to the call of Christ?

It's what it's always been: a deception. Do you know that the root of the word "deception" is "cept?" It is an underlying meaning of "taking" something not rightfully yours. It's "stolen understanding." Your revelation, your truth, is STOLEN. The opposite, "conception" is like "birth, understanding, or the beginning of something."

If He came now and set that clear line to separate you from your enemy, would you be on the right side of the cloud?

Jesus is our separation from the enemy. But we have to be on the right side. We must be sincere in our pursuit of Him. Pretending to be right in your sight may fool the world, but you are the one truly fooled. Justifying your position, "you're saved," Jesus knows your heart; yes, He does. That should terrify some of us. He truly knows our hearts.

To quote Jack Graham again, in his book, *A Man of God,* he says, "The only way to make a truly lasting difference is to change hearts, and that happens one heart and one life at a time."

Chapter 15

Dust and Ashes

It is better to operate from a place of victory, not give power to the current situation, but from the victory given to us at the cross, acknowledging the situation we're in and going through it knowing we have already been given victory over it.

I always hear the much-given, albeit good advice, "Pick your battles," which is wonderful advice. I've learned, though, that storms are a different story. The storm seems to choose us. Doesn't it? Most people don't go out looking for a storm, and if they see it coming, usually, if you're smart, you take shelter so you are not injured. That will preach.

But we don't necessarily invite the storm.

Nevertheless, we are subject to the stirring and the wind, and the loss and even to the damage. Fortunately, we are also given the recovery and restoration from the storms. But we never come out of them the way we went in. We shouldn't.

This "fear storm" we're living in is full of subliminal messages of deception. It's one of the weapons the enemy is using right now. If you don't believe me, turn the news on and look at just the graphics displayed behind the news articles and captions, and you will quickly see that the imagery displayed is those of panic, unrest, and anger. Colors like red and black, and pictures of distraught nurses, doctors, fires, ambulances, sirens, etc. The enemy using something we see to deceive us is not new, is it?

Adam and Eve were so deceived by something they saw that they chose deception over oneness and communion with God; after having known only oneness with Him, they sought something more.

How can this be?

The bible tells us that there is nothing new under the sun.

> "What has been will be again,
> what has been done will be done again;
> there is nothing new under the sun."

Ecclesiastes 1:9 (NIV)

In times of trouble and seeming uncertainty, there is always one constant: Jesus. God always brings a deliverer up.

> "And the Lord will deliver me from every evil work and preserve me for His heavenly kingdom. To Him be the glory forever and ever. Amen!"

2 Timothy 4:18 (NKJV)

Jesus is our deliverer, and He wants to deliver us from more than just the "threat" of an infection. He wants to accomplish a more individual work in each of us so that we rise out of the smoke around us and become burning flames—His burning ones.

I set a fire the other day. My mom was there "supervising." She was visiting for Mother's Day. We were working on unpacking in the new house. I'm still BLOWN AWAY at God's perfect goodness and provision. I wanted to burn away all the documentary evidence of things that had been burdening me, old burdens, old paperwork that reminded me of injuries and bondages we've endured over the years, mainly medical records, bills, etc. I just wanted to burn them.

But the fire, something about the fire was ministering to me. I watched the fire die out as I covered it to seal out the oxygen, but it kept smoking for hours. Interested, I opened the lid, stirred the ashes with a small wooden stick, and shifted them around to see where the smoke was coming from.

The wind caught it, and the fire ignited right back up. The fire grew as the wind blew, and the ashes were stirred. The Lord showed me something so beautiful. I thought how amazing it was that what seemed like only a pile of dust and ashes could be reignited into a burning flame with just a stir and a brush of fresh wind!

How that wooden stick reminded me later of the cross, brought me to tears, and the soft wind, the wind of the Holy Spirit breathing new life, Jesus.

Have you ever felt like nothing but a pile of ashes? You burned for Jesus but couldn't get the flame to spark and you felt like your prayers were going up in smoke. Were they catching God's attention? Where was His response? When will He send the Holy Spirit to reignite that flame that once burned so fiercely? My soul longed for Jesus. The smoke represented the longing.

I stared at the pile of dust and ashes and was reminded of the scripture that says to "repent in dust and ashes."

What does it mean to repent in dust and ashes?

Yes, it's a mourning, but I realized something gazing at that pile of ashes. Our flesh needs to die in the fire. We will die in a fire one way or another—the fire of eternal damnation or the fire of the Holy Spirit.

There's a song out now that says, "I want to be tried by fire, purified, take whatever You desire, Lord, here's my life."

I had been in a "purification" season for a while before the first time I heard this song, and when I heard it, honestly, I worried about the people singing it. Did they know what they were asking for? Purification is not easy. The season where God, The Holy Spirit, burns off of you everything that looks like flesh is painful. But this purifying fire is fulfilling.

The thing about this burning is that it hurts, but it feels good. Explaining this is hard, I guess. It's like you come to a place where you know the fire you're in is one where God is with you. And He is making you into someone beautiful, and He's putting in you just everything you need to come out of it: a new creation.

We often search for what is convenient and what is fulfilling to our flesh, and the gospel is not convenient to the flesh. That's why the bible says to "deny your flesh" and "take up your cross and follow Me." (Matthew 16:24, NKJV)

This made the Pharisees mad at Jesus; what He represented inconvenienced them. After He raised Lazarus from the dead, they said:

"If we leave Him alone like this, everyone will believe."

John 11:48 (NKJV)

They saw the power that He has, and for the sake of convenience, they sought to kill Him. If only they could have understood the love, the wholeness, the renewing that was offered, and the power of the Holy Spirit.

What a deception. The world we live in is a fallen, deceived world.

2 Timothy 4:3-5 (NKJV) says,

"For the time will come they will not endure sound doctrine, but according to their own desires, because they have itching ears, they will heap up for themselves teachers, and they will turn their ears away from the truth and be turned aside to fables. But you be watchful in all things, endure afflictions, do the work of an evangelist, fulfill your ministry."

Also 1 Timothy 4:1-2 (NKJV) says,

"Now the Spirit expressly says that in the latter times some will depart from the faith giving heed to deceiving spirits and doctrines of demons speaking lies in hypocrisy, having their own conscience seared with hot iron."

Jesus is the only way to the Father. If I am a Christian, then I must believe this. But honestly, I feel like a lot of times, we live like a bunch of sellouts, selling out for convenience, selling out for pride or arrogance, selling out for greed or covetousness. Selling out because we've convinced ourselves that something we see is more powerful than Jesus, than our Creator, or has more to offer us than the God of heaven and earth Himself.

And we are only as loyal to God as He is convenient.

God wants to raise us from the ashes and reignite the flame that once burned so brightly. To set His church ablaze so that the fire cannot be contained.

Jeremiah 20:9 says,

"Like a fire shut up in my bones…" (NKJV)

Luke 3:16 says,

"He will baptize you with the Holy Spirit and Fire." (NKJV)

Baptize with fire?

We've heard baptism in water, washing away of sins. The Holy Spirit Baptism is the baptism of fire, where we begin to burn with passion for Him, His kingdom, and His desires.

I just want to be right with Him. I know that whatever HE wants to do inside me is for my good and His glory. Who am I to say "no" to Him? What will it take for us to listen to His call and desire Holiness, desire to be close to Him, desire to live lives fulfilled by His goodness?

He's offering us wholeness.

Dust and ashes.

Repent. What does it mean to repent? I searched for this definition. It caught my heart. Listen to it:

"The full meaning of repentance, according to Jewish doctrine, is clearly indicated in the term "teshubah" (lit. "return"; from the verb שוב)[1]

To Return!

"The Hebrew meaning" implies: (1) All transgression and sin are the natural and inevitable consequence of man's straying from God and His laws (comp. Deut. xi. 26-28; Isa. i. 4; Jer. ii. 13, xvi. 11; Ezek. xviii. 30). (2) It is man's destiny, and therefore his duty, to be with God as God is with him. (3) It is within the power of every man to redeem himself from sin by resolutely breaking away from it and turning to God, whose loving-kindness is ever extended to the returning sinner. "Let the wicked forsake his way, and the unrighteous man his thoughts: and let him return unto the Lord, and he will have mercy upon him; and to our God, for he will abundantly pardon" (Isa. lv. 7; comp. Jer. iii. 12; Ezek. xviii. 32; Joel ii. 13). (4) Because "there is not a just man upon earth, that doeth good, and sinneth not" (Eccl. vii. 20; I Kings viii. 46), every mortal stands in need of this insistence on his "return" to God." [1]

> "It is within the power of every man to redeem himself from sin by resolutely breaking away from it and turning to God, whose loving-kindness is ever extended to the returning sinner."

This is good. What an encouragement.

God's kindness is what leads us to repentance. Conviction is the kindness and mercy of Christ. It is the invitation of your Creator to become closer to Him, to know Him deeper, and to become more like Him.

I want to say something about that description from the Jewish encyclopedia; it says it is within the power of every man to redeem himself, but we know Jesus offers us redemption; the power of Christ draws us unto Him, but it is our responsibility to turn away, resolutely break away from sin and turn to God.

Why is repentance such a slow turn for many of us? I think it's because of deception.

We don't want to be inconvenienced by "having to live holy."

But God is not trying to make me live a certain way. He's attempting to get us to accept the way of life we were created to live in, the only one that will truly be fulfilling, the path designed by HIM, by God Himself; what other way can I go?

"Lord, to whom *shall we go? You have* the *words of eternal life*" John 6:68 (NKJV)

Our enemy, once a beautifully adorned angel in heaven, was so deceived that he saw his beauty; he worshiped himself and thought everyone else should worship him, too.

Read Ezekiel 28:11-19 (NIV):

"The word of the Lord came to me: "Son of man, take up a lament concerning the king of Tyre and say to him: 'This is what the Sovereign Lord says:

'You were the seal of perfection,
full of wisdom and perfect in beauty.
You were in Eden,
the garden of God;
every precious stone adorned you:
carnelian, chrysolite and emerald,
topaz, onyx and jasper,
lapis lazuli, turquoise and beryl.
Your settings and mountings were made of gold;
on the day you were created they were prepared.
You were anointed as a guardian cherub,
for so I ordained you.
You were on the holy mount of God;
you walked among the fiery stones.
You were blameless in your ways
from the day you were created
till wickedness was found in you.
Through your widespread trade
you were filled with violence,
and you sinned.
So I drove you in disgrace from the mount of God,
and I expelled you, guardian cherub,
from among the fiery stones.
Your heart became proud
on account of your beauty,
and you corrupted your wisdom

because of your splendor.
So I threw you to the earth;
I made a spectacle of you before kings.
By your many sins and dishonest trade
you have desecrated your sanctuaries.
So I made a fire come out from you,
and it consumed you,
and I reduced you to ashes on the ground
in the sight of all who were watching.
All the nations who knew you
are appalled at you;
you have come to a horrible end
and will be no more.'"

He forgot or disregarded that he had a Creator who created him with that beauty. Not only did this pride deceive the enemy, but it also deceived a third of the angels in heaven to where they fell.

Read Revelation 12:9 (NIV),

"The great dragon was hurled down—that ancient serpent called the devil, or Satan, who leads the whole world astray. He was hurled to the earth, and his angels with him."

Read Luke 10:18 (NIV),

He replied, "I saw Satan fall like lightning from heaven."

Read Isaiah 14:12 (NIV),

"How you have fallen from heaven,
morning star, son of the dawn!
You have been cast down to the earth,
you who once laid low the nations!"

Who could willingly, after having been immersed in God's glory and wonder and presence, choose damnation and eternal separation from God?

Is it interesting to you that Jesus, in Luke chapter 10 after the disciples see that even the demons are subject to them in Jesus' name, that He refers to Tyre and Sidon? Then in Ezekiel 28, in the description of Satan falling from heaven, God uses this to bring the word to the king of Tyre, how he was lifted up because of his own wisdom. Then, Jesus says to His disciples,

"Woe to you Chorazin! Woe to you Bethasaida! For if the mighty works which were done in you were done in Tyre and Sidon, they would have repented long ago sitting in sackcloth and ashes!"

Luke 10:13 (NKJV)

He tells them,

"Behold, I give you authority to trample on serpents and scorpions and over all the power of the enemy."

Luke 10:19 (NKJV)

O Jesus, Your word is AMAZING.

He says how He turned the beauty of Satan into ashes. But for us, though we are nothing but ash, He brings beauty out of us and ignites the fire within us. Dust and ashes. He is inviting us to repent so we can come to Him, where we walk in this GOD-given authority to trample over every enemy threat!

Satan has fallen with his demons and is nothing but ash. Nothing can hurt us when we operate with the fire of the Holy Spirit. I don't want to exclude Jesus' comment here; He says not to rejoice in this, "that the spirits are subject to you, but rather rejoice that our names are written in heaven." It is a more glorious thing that someone is delivered out of their bondage and their names written in heaven than that a demon was subject to you. They are subject to the Name of Jesus Christ. Let's not be confused. God is enough, and anything that tries to convince you otherwise is deception coming to destroy your soul.

What concerns me for this time is that we will leave this season and go back into our lives and forget our Deliverer, our Redeemer who held us, brought us through, and even blessed us the whole time—providing, teaching, and just being more than enough in every way.

May we not ever look at the beauty and the work of God Himself around us and think for a second we are to receive the glory for it.

May we long for and receive the stirring of the cross that calls to us and bids us to come into His loving arms.

The cross from where Jesus' arms were held wide open, nailed wide open, His heart exposed, bleeding out, and pleading with the Father that He would forgive us. Do you think it was not within the power of Jesus to get down off that cross? He chose to stay on the cross for you, for me. The cross is our invitation to repent; it is the kindness and mercy of Christ that leads us to repentance.

May we allow the wind of the Holy Spirit to breathe on us and reignite the blazing fire that once burned inside us so contagiously. May we be open to the individual work God wants, and may we rise into the specific calling.

May we not be deceived by fleshly passions or the lies of these last days.

O Jesus. May we, Your bride, be awake and found watching for our Master when He returns for us.

> "Blessed are those servants whom the master, when he comes, will find watching."

Luke 12:37 (NKJV)

May we be consumed with compassion and kindness for each other.

2 Peter 3:9-10 (NKJV) says,

> "The Lord is not slack concerning His promise, as some count slackness, but is longsuffering toward us, not willing that any should perish but that all should come to

repentance."

2 Peter 2:14-18 (MEV) says,

"Therefore, beloved, since you are waiting for these things, be diligent that you may be found by Him in peace, spotless and blameless. Keep in mind that the patience of our Lord means salvation, even as our beloved brother Paul has also written to you according to the wisdom given to him. As in all his letters, he writes about these things, in which some things are hard to understand, which the unlearned and unstable distort, as they also do the other Scriptures, to their own destruction. You therefore, beloved, since you know these things beforehand, beware lest you also fall from your own firm footing, being led away by the deception of the wicked. But grow in the grace and knowledge of our Lord and Savior Jesus Christ. To Him be glory, both now and forever. Amen."

May we remember and accept the invitation to repent and become the people, the bride that You so passionately call us to be.

"Now, therefore," says the Lord,
"Turn to Me with all your heart,
With fasting, with weeping, and with mourning."
So rend your heart, and not your garments;
Return to the Lord your God,
For He is gracious and merciful."

Joel 2:12-13 (NKJV)

Let us remember Who we are serving and Whose children we are.

"Fear not o land, be glad and rejoice, for the Lord has done marvelous things." Joel 2:21 (NKJV)

"And it shall come to pass that whoever calls on the name of the Lord shall be saved." Joel 2:32 (NKJV)

We see the day coming; we repent, the Spirit comes, we are

refreshed, and the power of God moves.

> "In Him we were also chosen, having been
> predestined according to the plan of Him who works
> out everything in conformity with the purpose of His
> will, in order that we, who were the first to put our hope
> in Christ, might be for the praise of His glory. And you
> also were included in Christ when you heard the message
> of truth, the gospel of your salvation. When you believed,
> you were marked in Him with a seal, the promised Holy
> Spirit, who is a deposit guaranteeing our inheritance until
> the redemption of those who are God's possession—to the
> praise of His glory."

Ephesians 1:11-14 (NKJV)

What triggers the receipt of an inheritance is the death of the testator. Since Jesus was the testator, His death on the cross triggered our right to receive our inheritance now. As soon as He died on the cross, we gained access to the right to receive our inheritance.

We have an inheritance on the Earth during this life. We know the scripture,

> "I have come that you may have life and that life more
> abundantly."

John 10:10 (NKJV)

There is a fullness offered to us while we are living that we need to walk in, so His glory is shown through us.

> Ephesians 1:17-18 (NKJV) says, "That the God of our Lord
> Jesus Christ, the Father of glory, may give to you the spirit
> of wisdom and revelation in the knowledge of Him, the
> eyes of your understanding being enlightened; that you may
> know what is the hope of His calling, what are the riches of
> the glory of His inheritance in the saints."

Because we are called and sealed, we can know the hope that lies within our calling, and the riches of His glorious inheritance in the

86

saints. This is not about just us living out fullness, but about the souls that populate heaven, because when they see and hear us, they see and hear Him, and want that same favor, mercy, grace and abundant life.

So, we, as a body, are also His inheritance.

"That I may see the benefit of Your chosen ones,
That I may rejoice in the gladness of Your nation,
That I may glory with Your inheritance."

Psalm 106:5 (NKJV)

"To them God willed to make known what are the riches
of the glory of this mystery among the Gentiles: which
is Christ in you, the hope of glory." Colossians 1:27 (NKJV)

Chapter 16

Across the Sky

Have you ever suddenly remembered a dream, and the entirety of the dream played in your mind for a second? I had a moment recently where I remembered a dream this way.

There were two people, on, if you can imagine, a metal cord stretched across the sky. It was a blue sky. The clouds brushed across it and there were these two people in the middle of the wire crossing the sky. The second person held on to the first person but as they reached the middle the second person saw how high they were and began to panic. He was too scared to go any further and he called out for a rescuer.

The rescuer came connected to a parachute to take the second guy down. As the first person looked on at them going back down, he just shook his head as if to say, "You would have been fine, you were safe, you would have crossed." I thought, if only he had stayed, he could have crossed the sky.

It got me thinking of when we are in situations where we find ourselves thinking in our minds that we are unsafe, or we think we are unstable, and we are tempted or even convinced to call out for a rescuer and let go. We give up our path for one that "feels" safer to us.

As I looked at the two of them, I could see that as long as he held on to him, he would have been fine, and he could have crossed the sky. The first person did all the work; the second only had to hold on.

I have prayed the last few weeks for encouragement because I just see things that, when I look at them, bring a wave of unrest and discouragement and even instill a sense of insecurity; by that, I mean "un-safeness." I know what to do. It's pray. Not just praying but staying in a continual state of communion with Jesus. A continual "holding on to" Jesus.

The second man was out where he had never been before and made it halfway across the sky. He was safe the whole time, but when he looked at his surroundings, being so high in the sky, he felt unsafe, and panic gripped his heart and stopped him from going any further.

I've said and prayed that I wanted everything offered on the cross. Jesus Christ, the Messiah, came and died for me on the cross to give me a gift. This gift wasn't a single gift but rather a lifetime of treasures that I would get to walk out and discover in Him as I journey here on earth. This is the inheritance, but He didn't just give them to me to have, He gave them to me so I would use them. The treasures are not given to be kept hidden and stored away. He wants us to operate in the gifts and the fullness provided at the cross, and His designed purposes for us.

Our gifts and callings are so beautifully unique. After the Holy Spirit fell in the upper room (Acts 2:3), the bible says that divided tongues appeared over each of them, and they each heard in their native language. Acts tells us that people from every nation were there. That same chapter lists the different nations they were all from. People from every nation were there together.

"Now there were staying in Jerusalem God-fearing Jews from every nation under heaven. When they heard this sound, a crowd came together in bewilderment, because each one heard their own language being spoken." Acts 2:5-6 (NIV)

I think this represents that the gifts fall individually on each of us, but the message is one message: the fullness offered in Jesus Christ! They each received an individual outpouring but were all together to accomplish one thing. There weren't individual separate missions in the upper room. Their goal was that salvation, and the infilling of the Holy Spirit would come to all.

Peter, when he explained what was happening, said:

"Therefore, let all the house of Israel know assuredly that

God has made this Jesus, whom you crucified, both Lord and Christ (our salvation and our sovereign king)."

"Now when they heard this they were cut to the heart and said to Peter and the rest of the apostles and brethren: Men, what shall we do? Then Peter said to them, "Repent and let every one of you be baptized in the name of Jesus Christ for the remission of sins; and you shall receive the gift of the Holy Spirit. For the promise is to you and your children and to all who afar off AS MANY AS THE LORD OUR GOD WILL CALL."

Acts 2:36-39 (NKJV)

"AS MANY AS THE LORD OUR GOD WILL CALL!"

This is what I hear the Lord saying: "The projection of Hope the world is looking for and needs, by the way, is a body that dwells together in unity and allows the gifts to operate fully, individually and functioning together. This is what will attract the masses. The beauty of this diversity. Not a diversity in belief systems, but a diversity in giftings. The body, men, women, children, mother, business owner, teenager, leader, and layman all access the fullness offered to them on the cross and operate from that foundation of fullness, accomplishing one work: salvation and infilling of the Holy Spirit to the fullness of Christ."

This is when the body will attract the masses. This is when the picture comes together.

Wisdom says to allow the giftings to operate together. We are all so uniquely designed. I think He also wants to caution us, especially if you are a leader, to caution you of the tendency to compare yourselves to one another.

The bible says we are unwise to compare ourselves to others. Jesus is our measuring stick, not one another.

2 Corinthians 10:12 (NKJV) says,

"For we dare not class ourselves or compare ourselves with those who commend themselves but they, measuring themselves by themselves, and comparing themselves among themselves, are not wise."

Comparison takes the focus off what God is doing and has placed inside of you. You make yourself a judge of your brother or sister, considering their gift as something that is either inferior or superior to your own.

Divided tongues appeared over each one of them. Our God, the Creator of the universe, can certainly place a perfectly individualized calling and gifting and purpose inside of you, and what a waste of time comparison is.

Remember Ephesians 1:11 (NIV),

"In Him we were also chosen, having been predestined according to the plan of Him who works out everything in conformity with the purpose of His will."

We can't look down or around, and if we do, if we don't look up quickly and hold on to Jesus when we give up too soon, we let go too soon, and we miss out on crossing the sky.

This is one of the tragic results of comparison. You feel like you're either not measuring up or pouring out too much, and you want to give up. If we hold on to Him, He has everything we need with Him! Everything. Our fullness is in Jesus and comes as we hold onto Him.

So, the man called for the rescuer, and the rescuer came and took him down, but he would have been fine as long as he had held on. The first guy looked at him, like, "Why did you let go and leave? You could have crossed the sky."

For you church leader, if you find yourself out there hanging on, scared, and maybe you want to call for the rescuer, know this: the rescuer will come, and you will be safe, but as long as you are holding onto Jesus, you are never in danger.

Don't miss out on crossing the sky.

Hang on.

I asked the Lord for confirmation of what to say with this devotion, and the scripture He showed me is Luke 6:12 (NIV):

"And if you have not been faithful in what is another man's, who will give you what is your own? "No servant can serve two masters; for either he will hate the one and love the other, or else he will be loyal to the one and despise the other. You cannot serve God and mammon."

He said, you can't serve God's purpose and your own agenda at the same time.

The scripture goes on to say how He knows our hearts. Don't look around you. It's just you and Him and what He wants to do in and through you. Let Him do the work in you so He can accomplish the work through you.

Psalm 17:15 (NKJV) says,

"As for me, I will see your face in righteousness; I shall be satisfied when I awake in Your likeness."

Not in the likeness of some person, brother or sister, pastor or minister, but in HIS likeness. He is the measuring stick.

I'll end by saying this: I had been praying recently, and I finished the prayer "In Jesus' Name, Amen," and I wrote the question down, "What all does it mean when I say, 'In Jesus' Name?'"

That carries so much weight. "In Jesus' Name," and I think we say it so often, just so much out of habit, that we should be reminded of the power in the Name of Jesus.

The bible shows that when we say, "In The Name of Jesus," we are evoking and agreeing with all that His name encompasses, and so I want to list out so we are reminded of just some of the things the name of Jesus carries with it.

We can utterly rely on Jesus, His sacrifice to His victory, to now reigning King, He is our righteousness, Jesus is our freedom, our standard, our strong tower, our refuge, our strength, our enduring hope forever, our sustaining grace.

In Him, all fullness dwells.

He is the hope of glory, the weighty glory of the Father.

Jesus is the truth and the way and the life. "In Him we live and move and breathe and have our being."

He is our direction and our lighted path.

He is our peace, the Prince of Peace.

In Him is our victory.

He has all things under His feet.

He is the head of all principality and power.

He is our reconciliation, life, abundant life, and healing.

He is mercy, He is our deliverer, He is our protection, our foundation.

He is our covering, home, safe place, and surrounding grace.

He gives us wisdom, He is wisdom, and He gives us soundness of mind.

He is perfect love.

And I'm sure I'll find Him to be all of this and even more as I live.

I want to encourage you not to compare your gift and calling with others today. Let's embrace each other and celebrate the diversity in the body, the diversity of the gifts, callings, and the body that the Lord has called according to His purpose. Let's celebrate His purpose together. I want to encourage you, if you feel like letting go because maybe you panicked, don't. God says, hang on, I got you, you are safe.

Chapter 17

His Love Speaks

a Better Word

This world has nothing to offer us except the opportunity to bring His love to those around us and those falling to the devil's deception. My heart is broken today because I know the enemy is still having His way in so many lives, and God's people aren't responding.

But I declare that His body is stirring, and you will respond. I pray you will hear His love speak. You will listen to His love speaking when you face whatever you face. I pray our ears are more tender to Him than the enemy's lies.

The devil's roars are loud, but His love still speaks a better word. His promise to us is redemption. His promise is peace. His promise is power. His promise is His presence.

Our enemy, the only enemy we have, is Satan. There is no other opponent. "We do not wrestle against flesh and blood." If they are flesh and blood, they are not your enemy.

The devil whispers to you, and you think it's your own feelings.

"They don't get it."

"I'm too tired to fight."

"I'm done."

"I don't even care anymore."

"I'm just over it."

But you know in your spirit it isn't true.

What you feel is such overwhelming disappointment that your prayers weren't answered, or still have not been answered.

"How could He allow me to face what I have faced?

How could He allow that to happen in my life?"

"How could He allow such trauma, devastation, and disappointment?"

Maybe you were misjudged or felt like, "They couldn't take 5 minutes to genuinely care about what I was going through?" I felt all of these things.

I am a believer. I know His truth. I know His power. I've seen His power. I am a child of God. Healing is the children's bread. And I felt overwhelming disappointment that my prayers were not answered. But what I was hurt about was that the one thing that I had been believing for years was not happening. It seemed that the opposite happened. And things got worse.

Oh, believer, can't you see that the devil is a master of deception? He is the father of lies. "Because you see it, that is proof that it is subject to change." A friend of mine told me this regarding the MS diagnosis and the symptoms I was having. She said, "It's not going to be this way forever. If you can see it, is subject to change."

Her words are written in my spirit, and I know the truth in those words. Faith is the substance of things hoped for, the evidence of things unseen. Because you believe in it, it proves that it will change. "Your faith has made you well." The moment they believed, they were made well.

When the enemy gets us not to believe and to enter into doubt, we begin to back out of the awareness of His presence, and this is where we fall. We start to go back to familiar things, to drinking, smoking, drugs, relationships, whatever.

All in search of what?

Can you identify what you are really looking for?

I sought assurance that the things I was praying for would be answered. I needed peace in believing in Him for His answer. Because I kept not seeing it, because I couldn't see it, I began to doubt, and the doubt filtered what I saw Him doing. It was filtered with doubt. When things started to change, there was still a filter of doubt. Doubt leads to separation from His presence, and that is where we fall.

My answer was only going to be found in Him. In Him, we have peace. "These things I have spoken, that you may have peace in Me." (John 16:33)

This is what He says. Where is what you are looking for going to be found? It's not going to be found in a drug. It's not going to be found in a bottle. It's not going to be found in a relationship. It will only be found in Jesus; He is our hope.

"Now may the God of hope fill you with all joy and peace in believing…" Romans 15:13 (NKJV)

In believing in Him, I have peace. The devil introduces doubt to get you out of peace so that if you believe in Him, if there is doubt, you stop believing. That is his goal.

When I was diagnosed with this toilet bowl of a disease, I heard the Lord tell me, "As fast as it came, it's going to leave." The initial flare came on over six months. So, I believed that over the following six months, it was going to go, because that is what I thought I heard. In my mind, that is what I reasoned as an acceptable understanding of what I believed I heard.

It has now been over four years. I still have symptoms, and my healing has not manifested. Now I have a choice. Stop believing or stand.

The only place I have ever found peace is in Jesus. He is my stronghold. My healing has not manifested yet, but I believe He is my healer, and I will continue to stand on that truth. The enemy will try to get you out of peace by introducing doubt, but we must stand. "What are you O, great mountain? You will become a plain." (Zechariah 4:7, NKJV)

The Lord has spoken that better word. The one spoken by the sacrifice of Jesus Christ. This is the word that overcomes everything we will ever face. This is the word that is our foundation, our rock, our hope. It's Jesus. I will keep my eyes on Jesus. Nothing else will ever satisfy you. Not a relationship, not a drug, not money, not an acknowledgment, not vindication, or promotion. All of it is futile compared to the fullness offered by the presence of Jesus Christ in your life.

If you'd like to pray, say this:

Jesus, You alone satisfy, and I believe in Your better word. I pray that we will begin to be more sensitive to Your presence than any deception. My God, that we would see and hear You above all else. Forgive me, Lord, for ever doubting You. I accept Your grace and will stand in the peace of Your presence. In Jesus' Name, Amen."

Chapter 18

He Doesn't Care

The devil doesn't care if you're good or bad. He just wants you to be ineffective on the earth. I wonder even if he cares if you go to hell as long as you don't accomplish the work God called you to do on this earth. Taking the land you were called to inherit, living in the free promises we were given at our rebirth. (Saved by grace, sons of Abraham, Abraham's promises). Not to spite you, but to spite the Lord because he is offended.

The bible says we are not unwise to his devices (stealing, killing, and destroying; he is a liar and the father of it.)

1 Corinthians 3:3 (NKJV) is Paul talking to believers, saying,

"Where there are divisions among you, are you not acting like mere men?"

Some of Paul, some of Apollos, it doesn't matter. What matters is we love God. The enemy doesn't give two flips if you are "good" or "bad."

You can sit in church every week for your entire life and still go to hell. Do you enjoy being manipulated? Me either. But that's what we allow, and that is what he wants: to use us as pawns to destroy God's kingdom.

It's a futile thought if you understand God's Kingdom. It cannot be destroyed. We know that doesn't keep him from trying through his attacks—oppression, offenses, loss, etc.

God, who works all things out for the good of those who

love Him, does precisely that. He works ALL things out for our good. So, it is true that what the enemy meant for evil, God turns it around for our good. I'm convinced that the trials we face are only steps up in His kingdom that help us accomplish our purpose on this earth and enhance our impact on His kingdom.

Regarding living "good or bad," conviction comes from the love of the Holy Spirit. Condemnation comes from the rebuke of religion. One comes from natural, authentic love and then breeds freedom and, in turn, love again. The other breeds a race of cold-hearted, closed-off religion, tainted people stuck in divisions and spite and legalism, and puts chains on God's people.

Jesus knew and told us, "He who the Lord sets free is free indeed." You shall know the truth, and the truth shall set you free. What truth? HIS truth. His love. HE is the truth.

"He is the way, the truth, and the life." John 14:6 (NKJV)

Pharisees brought the woman caught in adultery to Jesus thinking He would condemn her, but what did He do? He IGNORED her accusers, and He set her free. Let's read it, John 8:1-11 (NKJV) says,

"Now, early in the morning He came again into the temple, and all the people came to Him; and He sat down and taught them. Then the scribes and Pharisees brought to Him a woman caught in adultery. And when they had set her in the midst, they said to Him, "Teacher, this woman was caught in adultery, in the very act. Now Moses, in the law, commanded us that such should be stoned. But what do You say?" This they said, testing Him, that they might have something of which to accuse Him. But Jesus stooped down and wrote on the ground with His finger, as though He did not hear. So when they continued asking Him, He [g] raised Himself up and said to them, "He who is without sin among you, let him throw a stone at her first." And again He stooped down and wrote on the ground. Then those who heard it, being[h] convicted by their conscience, went out one by one, beginning with the oldest even to the last. And Jesus was left alone, and the woman standing in the midst. When Jesus had raised Himself up and saw no one but the woman, He said to her, "Woman, where are those accusers of yours? Has no one condemned you?" She said, "No one, Lord." And Jesus said to her, "Neither do I condemn you; go and sin no more."

He told them, he who is without sin, cast the first stone – and one by one they left. His final word was to the woman,

"Neither do I condemn you, go and sin no more."

John 8:11 (NKJV)

Yes, He hates sin, but He hates sin because it separates us from His love! The whole purpose of our existence is to abide in His word and, thereby, in His love and spread that love around.

When we love Him, we start to feel convicted of sin as He brings us closer to Him. The closer we are, the more of the world that falls off us. He said if we walk in His light, we won't follow darkness because we see things from the perspective of His light! This is freedom.

"So Jesus said to the Jews who had believed Him, "If you abide in My word, you are truly My disciples, you will know the truth, and the truth will set you free." They answered Him, "We are offspring of Abraham and have never been enslaved to anyone. How is it that you say, 'You will become free'? "Jesus answered them, "Truly, truly, I say to you, everyone who practices sin is a slave to sin. The slave does not remain in the house forever; the son remains forever. So if the Son sets you free, you will be free indeed."

John 8:31-36 (ESV)

"Jesus answered, "I am the way and the truth and the life. No one comes to the Father except through me."

John 14:6 (ESV)

"For by grace you have been saved through faith. And this is not your own doing; it is the gift of God, not a result of works, so that no one may boast."

Ephesians 2:8-9 (ESV)

The enemy wants you trapped in an exhausted whirlwind of pointless, impactless activity. But God wants to give us freedom and grace extended. Our greatest impact comes from a place of rest and grace. Not an attitude of work. That's meant to wear you out and again render you ineffective.

When we understand grace, even the grace shown to us, we extend that grace to others and allow the Holy Spirit to do the convicting and not our words to bring condemnation to others.

Am I saying tolerate sin? No. I am saying don't allow anyone to make you feel condemned. Condemnation and conviction are completely different. Condemnation is cold and shameful and keeps you away from Jesus, and that's how it feels: cold, lonely, and separate from God. Conviction is freeing and warm and brings you closer to Jesus; that is how it feels.

The enemy knows if you get close to God, you will love Him, and you will experience and spread His love, and you might succeed in accomplishing His work on this Earth, which would keep the enemy off territory assigned for you to take.

When the enemy attacks, we threaten some advancement he is trying to make. You might be on the verge of a breakthrough in some area of your life, and it seems all hell breaks out, and you can't come up for air.

I am praying that the freeing, life-giving breath of the

Holy Spirit fills you up right now as you read, and you are encouraged that the armies of heaven are on YOUR side, and ALL this is working out for your good! And NOTHING can separate you from His love being able to access you.

You are a FORCE to be reckoned with! Get up! Take your land, baby! It's there for the grabbing.

He is on YOUR side, and WE WIN!

Conclusion / Prayer

Pray this if you would like:

Lord, I thank you that you are still healing today. I thank you that By Your Stripes, I am Healed! You accomplished the finished work on the cross. You took every disease, injury, and pain that would ever come to me and healed it all those years ago. I accept Your healing right now, even as I pray these words. I accept Your finished work. I accept You, my God. You are everything I need. I thank You, Lord, that You left NOTHING undone that You want to accomplish in me. I am completely Yours, and I fully submit to You, Lord. I ask that You have Your complete way in my mind, body, and soul right now, Lord, and I ask to be used by You for Your glory. In Jesus' Name, I pray, Amen.

The Lord is faithful to answer our prayers. He is still healing today. He unravels us like an onion, and layer by layer, He heals every broken piece, every injury, He restores. He really does give us beauty for ashes.

Isaiah 61 (NKJV) says,

61 "The Spirit of the Lord God is upon Me,
Because the Lord has anointed Me
To preach good tidings to the poor;
He has sent Me to [a]heal the brokenhearted,
To proclaim liberty to the captives,
And the opening of the prison to those who are bound;
² To proclaim the acceptable year of the Lord,
And the day of vengeance of our God;
To comfort all who mourn,
³ To [b]console those who mourn in Zion,
To give them beauty for ashes,
The oil of joy for mourning,
The garment of praise for the spirit of heaviness;
That they may be called trees of righteousness,
The planting of the Lord, that He may be glorified."

⁴ And they shall rebuild the old ruins,
They shall raise up the former desolations,
And they shall repair the ruined cities,
The desolations of many generations.
⁵ Strangers shall stand and feed your flocks,
And the sons of the foreigner
Shall be your plowmen and your vinedressers.
⁶ But you shall be named the priests of the Lord,
They shall call you the servants of our God.
You shall eat the riches of the Gentiles,
And in their glory you shall boast.
⁷ Instead of your shame you shall have double honor,
And instead of confusion they shall rejoice in their portion.
Therefore in their land they shall possess double;
Everlasting joy shall be theirs.

⁸ "For I, the Lord, love justice;
I hate robbery [c]for burnt offering;
I will direct their work in truth,
And will make with them an everlasting covenant.

⁹ Their descendants shall be known among the Gentiles,
And their offspring among the people.
All who see them shall acknowledge them,
That they are the posterity whom the Lord has blessed."

¹⁰ I will greatly rejoice in the Lord,
My soul shall be joyful in my God;
For He has clothed me with the garments of salvation,
He has covered me with the robe of righteousness,
As a bridegroom decks himself with ornaments,
And as a bride adorns herself with her jewels.
¹¹ For as the earth brings forth its bud,
As the garden causes the things that are sown in it to spring
forth,
So the Lord God will cause righteousness and praise to
spring forth before all the nations."

Amen

Reference: http://www.jewishencyclopedia.com/articles/12680-repentance

REPENTANCE (Hebr. "teshubah"):

By: Kaufmann Kohler, Max Schlesinger

Bibliography:

2. Bousset, Religion des Judenthums, pp. 368 et seq.;

3. Claude Monteflore, Rabbinic Conceptions of Repentance, in J. Q. R. xvi. 209-257;

4. Singer, Isidore, Ph.D, Projector and Managing Editor. Entry for 'Repentance'. 1901 The Jewish Encyclopedia.

5. https://www.studylight.org/encyclopedias/eng/tje/r/repentance.html. 1901

6. Weber, Jüdische Theologie, Index.

Printed in the USA
CPSIA information can be obtained
at www.ICGtesting.com
CBHW051152181024
16013CB00006B/101